To Carol
Hope you enjoy
the book.
Wendy Bruce Thompson

Down And Almost Under

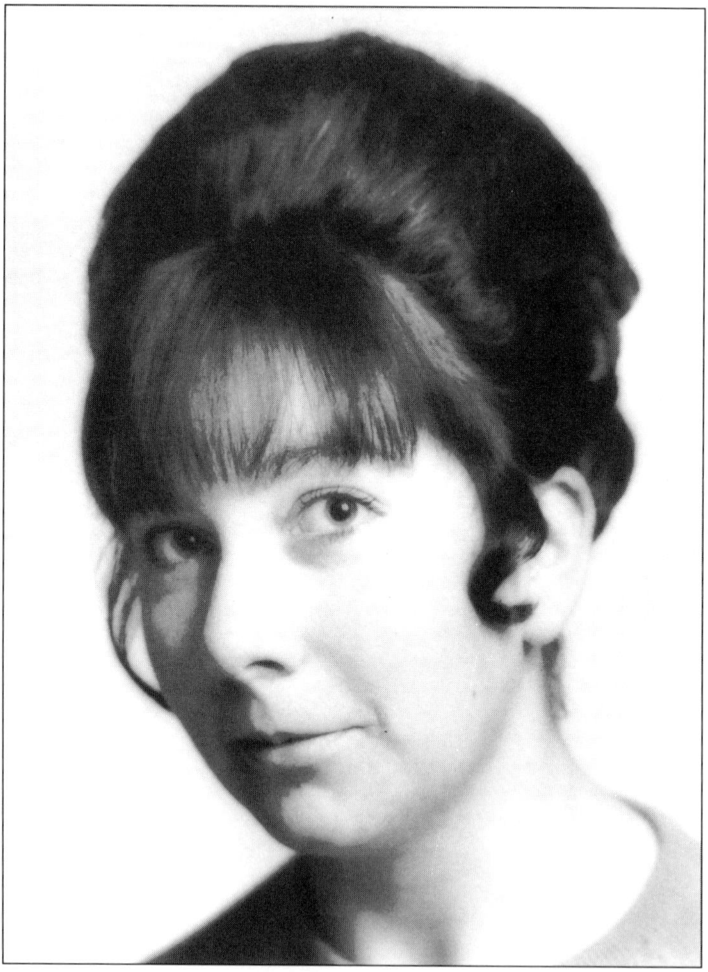

The author, early in 1973 before embarking for New Zealand.

Down And Almost Under

by

Wendy Brice Thompson

The Memoir Club

First published in 2000 by
The Memoir Club
Whitworth Hall
Spennymoor
County Durham

British Library Cataloguing in
Publication Data.
A catalogue record for this book
is available from the
British Library.

ISBN: 1 84104 016 9

Typeset by George Wishart & Associates, Whitley Bay.
Printed by Bookcraft (Bath) Ltd.

This book is dedicated
to the memory of

Les Franklin

Acknowledgements

MY GRATEFUL THANKS go to those friends and family members who sweet-talked, encouraged and eventually bullied me into writing this very personal account of the time I spent living in New Zealand.

I am indebted to my husband, who bought me the computer to type on and who put up with so many makeshift meals without (much) complaint. He also helped me check the proofs and did all sorts of clever technical things to the computer when it refused to co-operate. Thanks must also go to my son Adrian, who gave so freely of his advice and criticism and to the staff at the Alma Arms Public House, who laughed so uproariously at my old photographs.

Most of all I should like to thank through this book all those kind and generous people who took care of me while in New Zealand.

That's all, folks, let's go . . .

Contents

List of Illustrations ix

Introduction xi

Part One – The Greek Lady

Chapter I London, 1973 3

Chapter II Aboard the *Ellinis* 8

Chapter III Rotterdam and Bremerhaven 15

Chapter IV Kerry Goes Shopping in Las Palmas 21

Chapter V Crossing the Line 28

Chapter VI Perth, Melbourne and Sydney 37

Part Two – The Long White Cloud

Chapter VII Auckland – Gift of the Sea 49

Chapter VIII Philip, Mariana and Richard 63

Chapter IX New Year at Lake Taupo 78

Chapter X Waiheke Island 87

Chapter XI A Royal Visit to Auckland 92

Chapter XII Wellington 100

Chapter XIII The Return of Jan-Yves 109

Chapter XIV Doctors, Dentists, and Other Good Works 118

Chapter XV Goodbye to New Zealand 128

Epilogue 137

List of Illustrations

The author, early in 1973 before embarking for New Zealand . . . . Frontispiece

S.S. *Ellinis* 9

Crossing the Line 29

The author near Capetown 31

On board the ship en route to Melbourne. Kerry (centre) with two other passengers 38

Rangitoto Island, Auckland Harbour 52

From left to right, Philip, Les and Richard Franklin at the Savage Memorial, Auckland 54

The author's flat in Mount Albert, Auckland 59

The bank in Avondale where the author worked 64

The Franklins' home in Remuera, Auckland 74

Christmas Day 1973 75

Farewell dinner at the Franklins' 133

Mariana and Les Franklin 134

Introduction

DOWN AND ALMOST UNDER is the true story of the year that I spent living and travelling in New Zealand almost twenty-five years ago. It is based on journals and letters and was intended to be a personal account of a young woman's journey from teens to adulthood. If life was a dance, then I had all the steps to learn.

On re-reading my original drafts on the dawn of the new Millennium, what strikes me most is that the story is more of a social comment than a mere travelogue. The remarkable changes that have occurred since the events of the book took place have turned this tale into what is almost a piece of history.

Australia and New Zealand are now popular holiday destinations but in 1973 people still sailed to the other side of the world in search of new opportunities or adventure and some never expected to see England again.

A sexual revolution had taken place in the mid-sixties, but assuredly it had not yet reached the leafy suburbs of suburbia during the early seventies. Girls may have slept with their boyfriends but they didn't talk about it openly. We wore big hair-dos, lipsticks so pale that it made us all look as if we had anaemia, and clothes made of plastic. We knew it all and we knew nothing. Margaret Thatcher had not yet become the first woman leader of a British Political Party and the European Union was still referred to as the Common Market. Computers were mega-sized monsters that required half an office block for accommodation and were operated by clever folk in white coats. Colour television was still a novelty. No one had ever heard of *Star Wars* or *Luke Skywalker*, there was no such thing as the Internet, no one learned media studies and Tony Blair was still playing the guitar in his beat group. There were no mobile phones – in fact a telephone call to New Zealand was a major technical feat, requiring to be booked in advance.

So while Britain shivered through the winter of discontent in 1974, I played in the Antipodean sunshine and enjoyed a special and wondrous place – New Zealand, Land of the Long White Cloud.

PART ONE

The Greek Lady

CHAPTER I

London, 1973

IN 1974 THE QUEEN and I visited New Zealand.

Her Majesty went as Head of State to open the Commonwealth Games in Christchurch, while I, an overweight and mostly unappealing nineteen year-old, outraged my family and friends by purchasing a one-way ticket to Auckland and announcing that I was off to see the world – or more precisely the other side of it.

Looking back, I blame it all on Kate. She was my best and oldest friend and we'd been joined at the hip since we were eleven years old, when she grudgingly permitted me to crib her algebra homework. Neither of us would change the shade of her lipstick without first consulting the opinion of the other. That's the sort of friend Kate was.

She was late meeting me for lunch one day at our favourite pub in Bishopsgate, a not unheard-of event. This time, however, instead of anxiously scanning the incoming faces pouring through the door for their beer and lunch, I settled comfortably in my corner seat and brooded on what a pleasant thing it would be to emigrate. As usual, I'd used up my daily quota of calories by lunchtime and guilt reaction was setting in, so I consoled myself with a port and lemon, lavishly spread butter on to my chunk of French bread, and sat back to take serious stock of my achievements to date and my future prospects. I could see little virtue in living beyond the age of thirty. Having just celebrated my last teenage birthday, I was miserably convinced that if I didn't do something pretty dramatic very soon, then it would all be too late.

I had been working for a year in a boringly respectable bank, which was the last thing in the world that I wanted to be doing. By this time I was reluctantly coming to the conclusion that I was not intended to be a corporate high-flier. I had left school in a blaze of under-achievement, the greater part of my scholarly career having been taken up with avoiding things: history tests, maths tests, medicals and games. The one and only member of teaching staff who had anything nice to say about me was the drama mistress, a kindly and perceptive soul, who obviously recognised in me the talent that *I* knew was there; but hers was a lone voice among the chorus of disapprobation.

Suffice it to say that I was an adept at avoiding the unpleasant. Now life was promising to be very boring indeed and I was dangerously ripe for some excitement. New Zealand started to look more and more appealing.

Of course I wasn't completely unqualified. I could type and I made a perfect cup of tea and I had perfected a filing system that no-one else could fathom. Fondly, I kidded myself I was indispensable. I had a nodding acquaintance with the Opposite Sex and sometimes the Opposite Sex even noticed me. When they did, they usually got my name wrong. If they phoned, it was only to enquire the whereabouts/availability/telephone number of one of my more attractive girlfriends. I would give them the information they sought and be rewarded by being told I was a good mate.

However, I never gave up hope altogether of finding a man of my own and dragged myself to discos and clubs, where I spent most of the time dashing in and out of the loos. Constantly checking and re-checking my hair and my lipstick, and posing in front of the mirror to hold my stomach flat, I would only emerge when everyone else was paired off. Out on the dance floor, I was the one who sat and looked after the handbags. In the unlikely event of a boy approaching me for a dance, I would instinctively look over my shoulder, assuming they must be talking to someone else. If discos were bad, then parties were a nightmare for the queen of wallflowers. I became a compulsive collector of empty glasses and took refuge at the sink, up to my elbows in Fairy Liquid.

In an attempt to make myself more interesting, I attended poetry readings and hid behind a large pair of spectacles that I hoped made me look intelligent if I couldn't be pretty. I nourished dreams of becoming the next Virginia Woolf, read two novels a week and watched high-brow documentaries on television.

This was the current sad state of things one spring day when

Kate stood me up for lunch and it dawned on me that I needed a change of direction and a change of scene – urgently. It might have been easier to scour the 'sits. vac.' columns in the evening paper but that was too obvious for me. Always impulsive, I took the next morning off, took the bus to New Zealand House and came away happily armed with books, maps and the unswervable decision that New Zealand was the country for me. At this point I nurtured the delightful fiction of disembarking off the ship in Auckland and being obliged to fend off hordes of woman-hungry, hairy-chested and bare-kneed Kiwi males eagerly fighting over the little woman from the ol' country.

The reaction in the office when I announced my grand decision at afternoon coffee was consistently unfavourable.

'You'll be homesick!'

'You'll never find a decent job!'

'Where exactly *is* New Zealand anyway?'

While they were having their say, I unfolded a map and spread it across my desk. 'Here's New Zealand.' I pointed at two small blobs of red somewhere off the eastern seaboard of Australia. 'Te Aotearoa, the Land of the Long White Cloud,' I informed them glibly. Heavens though, it was such a long way!

Resolved that my declaration of independence was more than an empty gesture, I raided my piggy bank, cheerfully renounced chocolate and undertook to raise money for the fare for my southbound passage from Southampton to Auckland. I calculated that I would have sufficient funds to join the October sailing that year.

The reaction on the home front was not a happy one. I was an only child, trained to be an obedient daughter. Even if I could never aspire to being truly ladylike, gallivanting off to the other side of the world unchaperoned was definitely not the done thing.

I took a deep breath and prepared to weather the storm. My mother fussed and fretted like a tiresome *mama* in a Jane Austen novel.

'I can understand you wanting to travel dear, but does it have to be quite so far away?' She called upon each of her own friends in turn, and then on mine, to try and talk me out of it. She threatened to call in the Vicar, and I knew then that at last she was taking my proposed departure seriously. Hoping that love might prevail where reason had fallen on deaf ears, she paraded a motley collection of young men for my inspection. Mother made encouraging comments about these chinless wonders she had found Lord knows where. I politely took tea with them all, pitied my mother – and quietly continued with my packing.

Short of locking me away on a diet of bread and water, which she no doubt would have tried had I not been so much bigger than she, there was little she could do. Finally resigned to the fact that her ungrateful daughter was fleeing the nest, her resistance capitulated. She bought me a duvet and an expensive handbag.

I intended to be well prepared for my venture, so I visited the library, where I found a small selection of books on New Zealand wedged between Japan and Australia. I crammed the lot: the travels of Captain Cook, Pioneer Women and, just to be on the safe side, a weighty manual on sheep farming. Though I was never called upon to put it to the test, I fancied I might have had quite an aptitude for raising sheep.

Suddenly everyone had contacts in New Zealand. If I ever found time to look up all the cousins or their children or all the neighbours who had emigrated, I would never lack for company.

They gave me a good send-off at the bank. I had a card that was almost two feet tall that everyone had signed, and lots of presents, all small, easily packed and practical. We went out for a drink in the lunch hour and I got very tipsy. I was so hysterically giggly and weepy by turns that the barman thought I must be getting married.

'We get a lot of them in here like that,' he said glumly.

I bought cream cakes for everyone and tried to explain the technical merits of my precious filing system to one of the juniors. She stared at me blankly so I wrote it all down. The strain of my leaving and her new responsibilities proved too much for her on a Friday afternoon. She took refuge in the ladies for at least twenty minutes, accompanied by a couple of companions.

I was left marvelling at how necessary it was for sixteen year-olds to spend a penny in pairs.

Finally the great day arrived. My cabin trunk had been sent on well in advance. I had a huge suitcase destined for hold storage, and some hand luggage, including a generous supply of writing paper and some new exercise books. I was determined to start a journal and write lots of letters. As I didn't know anyone on the ship, writing home would give me something to do. I had bought a copy of *Papillon* at the bookstall to read on the train.

Kate and another girlfriend accompanied me to Waterloo. They marched one on each side of me along the platform, past carriages rapidly filling up with would-be sailors like myself: emigrant families, ex-pats returning home, tourists and experienced globe-trotters. I was both excited and cold with nerves.

At the head of the train we found an almost empty carriage.

'This will do.' I dumped my bags on the platform and opened the carriage door.

'Look, Wendy, it's not too late to change your mind. Are you really going to go through with this?' Kate asked me anxiously.

As usual I brazened it out. 'Of course it's too late. I'm committed. I know what I'm doing and anyway it won't be for ever.'

I managed to smile brightly at her and she refrained from further comment. As I said, Kate had known me a long time.

'Then you'd better get on. Don't forget to write.' She handed me a small, wrapped package. 'You can open that on the train.'

I scrambled aboard and stowed my bags above the seat. A good looking, sun-burnt young man sitting opposite looked up and smiled. I smiled back and Kate, peering in through the window, beamed with approval.

Whistles blew. I leaned out of the window, under a sign that said 'Caution. Do Not Lean Out of the Window.' The Southampton boat train pulled slowly out of the platform. I watched the two small figures receding from view. One raised a hand and waved a white hanky at me. I didn't think people actually waved hankies at departing trains any more – not outside of old movies.

I plonked down in my seat. *Papillon* remained untouched for the entire journey.

CHAPTER II

Aboard the *Ellinis*

IT WAS LATE AFTERNOON when the train arrived at Southampton docks in a chilly grey drizzle.

The shipping terminal and customs control were cheerful enough, though they resembled an enlarged cross-section of an anthill. Ants, however, we are led to understand, are intelligent, possess a clarity of purpose and actually know what they are doing. The assembled masses mustered in the terminus building gave no indication that they knew either individually or collectively what they were doing and appeared resigned to being shuttled from one set of officials to another.

All passengers were being issued with several cards of different colours and, from what I could gather, embarkation was permitted only when one was in possession of all the cards in the correct colour sequence. This was my first experience of embarkation procedures courtesy of Chandris Lines, but it was one to which I would become all too irritatingly familiar over the next few weeks. I clamped my ticket between my teeth, carefully stacked my bags under my arms like stabilisers, and staggered across the floor to join the shortest queue.

While I waited, I had my first view of the ship, berthed alongside. She was called *Ellinis*, which means Greek lady. In a previous life she had been the *Marapoza* and had done long service as a troop-carrier during the War. Some observers, more cynical than I, might declare she was a troop-ship still. I thought she was beautiful, vast and comforting, smartly turned out in a coat of fresh white paint with two white crosses marked on both blue funnels.

Seen though the none-too-clean windows of the customs building on a dreary English October afternoon, she was a magnificent ship. For better or worse, she would be my home for the next six weeks.

S.S. Ellinis.

Once on board, the confusion of the terminus building was repeated. Passengers shuffled uncertainly, children grizzled and clusters of stewards stood around in groups killing time in true Greek fashion.

I made a bee-line for one of the stewards and dropped my bags at his feet. He was shorter than I, with a greasy complexion, beautiful black curly hair and sloe eyes. His smart maroon livery was too tight for comfort but he smiled slowly at me and fixed his eyes deliberately on my breasts. I showed him my cabin number and he reluctantly lowered his eyes to examine it. Then he said something in Greek to the others and they laughed. I fixed a nasty little smile on my lips and waited.

He indicated that I should follow him and we set off down the first of many flights of stairs into the lower regions of the ship. There were ten decks on the *Ellinis* and naturally the cabin assigned to me was near the bottom. The steward carried the smaller of my bags while I struggled along with the larger one. In this manner we foot-slogged along miles of dark corridors and around countless corners. It smelt very stuffy but I learned later that ships are always stuffy below. This is preferable to the air-conditioning because when it is working full out, it turns the corridors into wind tunnels.

At last we came to a door that opened into a long, narrow cabin. It was wood-panelled and contained three sets of bunks. In the farthest corner was a vanity unit and a small mirror. Even with the lights on, it was depressing and gloomy.

A tiny elderly lady perched dejectedly on one of the lower

bunks. My noble Corinthian dumped my bag unceremoniously on the floor, leered at me and sidled out. I felt a great deal better after I had slammed the door behind him.

The old lady peered at me through a pair of thick glasses. She was wearing a hideously bold check skirt and a shabby fawn cardigan and her swollen fingers absently tugged at the top button. I sat down opposite her and told her my name. I had to repeat it because she was evidently hard of hearing. The poor old stick was pathetically confused because it turned out that her husband was in another cabin. She didn't know where it was and she had been given the top bunk to sleep in, which she couldn't possibly get into.

I checked the bunk numbers on her ticket and mine. Mrs Daisy Connolly, seventy-eight years old and arthritic, had been given the top bunk; myself, aged nineteen and built like a Rhine Maiden, the bottom bunk.

'We'll swop bunks, Mrs Connolly,' I hastened to reassure her. 'I'd prefer the top one anyway.' The old lady lay back and closed her eyes. The effort of walking down all the stairs and corridors had been too much for her. I left her in peace and ventured out to explore. I stalked the lower decks from bow to stern, peering into cupboards, pantries and shower rooms. Climbing upstairs, I discovered the Main Lounge, the Ballroom, the Outrigger Bar and the swimming pool. This was slightly larger than a bath tub. I promenaded the Promenade Deck in both directions, carefully counting the life boats. There didn't seem to be nearly enough.

My evaluation of the ship's life preservers was interrupted by a blast on the siren like the last trump. It was now completely dark and *Ellinis* was about to weigh anchor. There were no streamers or bands, merely a handful of well-wishers huddled in forlorn little groups on the quay, occasionally calling out to their loved ones. An equally small number of passengers leaned over the ship's rail to wave goodbye. Obviously the leave-taking of England was not breaking any hearts. The ship shuddered, blasted the siren again and, hauled by the tugs, drifted slowly away from the quayside. The lights of Southampton twinkled in the darkness and *Ellinis* was under way.

There seemed little point in remaining out on deck. It was too dark to see much and the indistinct blur of oil tanks wasn't the last sight I wanted of home. As soon as the ship reached open water, the wind became treacherous. Some young children stampeded past me. One fell flat on his face and the others ignored him. He started to howl but his friends pounded on up a metal companionway. I picked the small casualty up and dusted off his knees. Fortunately he had suffered no real damage.

'Don't run about like that,' I reprimanded. 'It's dangerous.'

To my own ears I sounded like someone's mother. The small boy scampered off in pursuit of the other children and I thankfully took refuge in the warmth of the ship's interior.

It took several wrong turnings before I found my cabin. I was soon to wish I hadn't. From inside came the sound of several voices raised in complaint. Out in the corridor an unhappy steward cowered under the verbal broadside of three angry females. Two, by the sound of it, were middle-aged and the third, the only one of the three I could actually see, was a gorgeously pretty blonde girl of about my age, shouting in an unmistakable Welsh accent. It was the young one who was making the most noise.

'I'm damn well not taking any bloody thing to the Baggage Room,' she bawled. 'I need *all* these bloody bags!'

'Well you can't keep them all in here; there's no room,' one of the other two women protested.

The steward muttered something about excess luggage being stored in the Baggage Room. Only one item might be retained in the cabin. In other words, take out what you need and everything else must be stored away. Access was permitted to the Baggage Room once a day and if you ran out of a spare pair of tights in the meantime, it was hard luck.

The blonde girl spotted me hovering outside. 'Are you in here as well?' she demanded.

'Yes.' (Unfortunately, I thought.)

'What?'

'I said yes. Look, I have a suggestion.' I pushed past the Greek obstruction in the doorway. He smelled of polo mints. Inside the cabin the three other women stared at me.

I began, 'As there are five of us and it's a six-berth cabin, there should be enough room for all of us to hang on to a little extra luggage in here.' I glanced at Polo Mints for verification. He looked almost grateful and shrugged.

'Okay. Why not?'

Another steward appeared. He was older than Polo Mints, with a bored, crumpled-up face like Robert Mitchum. The two men gabbled in rapid Greek while the blonde girl posed and pouted. She smiled encouragingly. The older steward suddenly noticed her properly and she smiled some more. His face lit up in anticipation and I could see him mentally falling to his knees in homage to this blonde goddess.

'Of course that will be all right. You may leave your bags in here.' His accent was delicious and I forgave him for overlooking the fact that it had been my suggestion. 'I'm Mike. If you should need anything, *anything at all*, ask for Mike.'

He finally acknowledged the rest of us and we were treated to a smile of sensual promise. He still managed to keep one eye on the siren in the corner.

'Actually there is something,' I said, remembering the old lady Daisy, still napping on her bunk. 'Mrs Connolly has been separated from her husband. Do you know where he is?'

Mike indicated with his thumb the door across the passage. He replied kindly, 'But he is just next door.'

With one more smouldering look at the blonde girl – I half expected him to kiss her hand – he turned away and was gone, Polo Mints at his heels.

'Ooh, well!' The two older ladies glared indignantly. The blonde girl ignored them and commandeered the wardrobe closest to her bunk. She flung open one of three large suitcases and began to empty its contents with the thoroughness of a dog digging up a favourite bone. Tee shirts, jeans, various bits of underwear and finally an unidentifiable piece of black lace – all went flying across the room to arrive in a heap on her bunk. Fascinated, I sat down to watch.

All the while she chattered non-stop – to me, presumably, as the most likely audience. Her name was Kerry Evans and she was going home to New Zealand. Home was Tauranga, a town on the east coast of North Island. She was buxom and very tall, with dark eyebrows and thick wavy blonde hair. This was Monroe with a Welsh accent. She was unfashionably shapely, with muscles as well as curves. As I discovered later, she was hopelessly vain, selfish, bossy, insecure and man-mad. She was to delight and exasperate me by turns but at our first meeting the only thing we had in common was that we both perpetually dieted.

Whereas I was quiet, Kerry could be heard coming a mile off. My nose was destined to be forever stuck deep in a book; Kerry's literary experience was limited to the instructions on a bottle of hair conditioner. Out of such unlikely material are friendships made. I loved and I hated her.

The Welsh accent that conjured up images of male voice choirs and *Under Milk Wood* had me stumped. Kerry was only too happy to explain at length how she had met this Welsh bloke in New Zealand, followed him back to Cardiff, and married him. Three years later she was divorced, twenty-one, and stony-broke. Her father had sent her the money for her fare home.

I was too polite to point out that for someone reputedly penniless, she appeared to have a remarkable supply of expensive lingerie. I jealously thought of my own unexciting wardrobe.

The two middle-aged women were sisters-in-law. Their husbands were brothers who were to be official adjudicators of the swimming events in the forthcoming Commonwealth Games. They were combining the trip with a once-in-a-lifetime holiday. Mentally I christened them Mrs Sarah and Mrs May.

They were an odd pair. The elder of the two, Mrs Sarah, was gaunt and bespectacled. She wore her long string of grey hair screwed back in a severe bun. There she perched on the edge of her bunk, bony knees pressed primly together and, although we were scarcely clear of Southampton Water, began a letter home. She talked as though she had swallowed a dictionary, speaking in short, clipped sentences and I have no doubt that the grammar of her letter was faultless.

Her sister-in-law, Mrs May, was as amply upholstered as Sarah was skinny. Her bottom protruded like a shelf and I swear a cup of tea could have balanced on it. She exuded motherly good will. Her tightly permed curls framed a jolly face, as rounded and shiny as the rising sun. Bright glossy red lipstick matched the frilly blouse she was wearing, that tried unsuccessfully to conceal her double chin. The buttons were only just holding their own in restraining the swell of her magnificent bosom.

Presently she kicked off her high heels and fumbled furtively under the pleats of her skirt to grapple with her suspenders. After peeling off one stocking, she stuck her foot up in the wash basin and proceeded to minister to the demands of her corns.

CHAPTER III

Rotterdam and Bremerhaven

FOUR DAYS OUT OF Southampton on a brilliant clear, bitingly cold day, I sat huddled out on deck, well wrapped up in my grey winter coat, boots and beret. A persistent headwind whipped up white horses on the sea and blew little tendrils of hair across my face.

In spite of the cold there were plenty of people outside. They were muffled deep in overcoats, some strolling up and down the deck singly or in pairs while others passed the time leaning against the ship's rail or watching the circling, screeching seagulls through binoculars. The *Ellinis* cruised sedately at a steady twelve knots, next port of call, Las Palmas.

Life on board had started to take on a regular daily routine. There was plenty to do for the energetic, like the two portly, heavy breathing individuals who had just trotted (it wasn't called jogging in those days) past me for the umpteenth time, clad in tracksuits and plimsolls. Six times around the Boat Deck equalled one mile.

For the less athletic there was the usual mixture of cruise entertainment: whist drives, slide shows, yoga, deck sports (also cabin sports, though these were not so widely advertised), debating groups and a never-ending round of amateur dramatics. An ocean voyage is a paradise for the star-struck, for, as there is usually a limited number of professional entertainers on board, the bulk of the cast for the weekly theatrical productions is made up of passengers.

The ones that were less than willing to make fools of themselves were artfully flattered or bullied into taking part. The talented, the enthusiastic and the downright hopeless – all were knocked into shape. The driving force behind all this wearisome activity was the Entertainments Officer, Jon Denis. This effete and second-rate poseur tolerated the efforts of his willing charges with a barely concealed impatience. He strutted around the Ballroom at rehearsals, a lithe golden man with sun streaked hair and a skimpy tee shirt that exposed his deep tan to best advantage. A heavy gold locket hung around his neck and he wore a large flashy wristwatch. A skilful dancer and a tireless organiser, he called us all 'love'. No one liked him.

He did have one thing in his favour: he wasn't Greek. I had decided I had a strong aversion to Greeks, and Greek stewards in particular. They were a lazy lot, oily, smooth-talking and never to be found when wanted. Sometimes downright comic, more frequently infuriating, the only decent one I had come across was Kerry's admirer, Mike. He was always pathetically eager to please, hovering around outside our cabin hoping for a glimpse – and possibly more – of the object of his affections. The lady in question alternately flirted with or ignored him. She could be quite nasty to the poor man and I told her so.

Within the close confines of the cabin the situation of the first day had thankfully subsided into an uneasy truce. Sarah and May still viewed Kerry with obvious disapproval of her clothes, loudness and cheek. Kerry complained to me non-stop about their stuffiness. Stuffy they weren't and Kerry was a silly girl, though not really bad. All the same, without me to mediate constantly between the two factions, the atmosphere could have been unbearable.

It was Daisy, the old lady, whom I felt sorry for. She was almost always to be found sitting unhappily on her bunk or outside in the passage, leaning with one spot-blemished hand on the wall to steady her. She rarely made it as far as the upper decks and the sunshine.

Her husband – 'him who is next door', as she called him – turned out to be a bad-tempered and petulant old man, who had long since renounced the power of speech in favour of unintelligible grunting. Each morning he poked his head around the door, often without the courtesy of knocking first, and then summoned his spouse to breakfast with a disagreeable noise somewhere between a snort and a growl. Daisy, who, as I have said, was hard of hearing – considering her marital circumstances, this was probably a blessing – would ignore him, so one of us had to relay the signal to her. The old misery never waited while she struggled painfully to her feet, but shambled off in the direction of the stairs. He always wore the same old pair of slippers but never put them on properly, so his heels overhung the backs and they flapped up and down as he walked. Daisy, poor soul, tottered obediently in his wake.

Aboard ships, as in hospitals, mealtimes are unquestionably the highlights of the day. There were three sittings for each meal. The first was for families and, to judge from some of the mess left on the tables, this must have been a bacchanalia of juvenile disorder. On our first evening, after Kerry had finally decided on what to wear, we joined the long queue outside the dining room. It was like lining up for school dinners. I had always detested queuing for anything and this occasion was no exception, but I had to eat so I waited with as much patience as I could muster.

The dining room was enormous and decorated like a tacky night-club in Essex. Stewards decked out in bow ties and crimson mess jackets stood like sentinels around the room. One detached himself from the others and came towards us.

He consulted the list in his hand and escorted Kerry to her table. He politely pulled out the chair for her while she turned and pulled a face at me behind his back. Unhurriedly he came back to me, inquired my name and pointed vaguely in the direction of the furthest corner of the room.

'Thank you *so* much,' I snapped.

I made my way over to a large round table and sat down in the one remaining empty chair. There were five people already seated, two couples and a girl. They all made a point of wishing me good evening. I mumbled a reply and took refuge behind the menu.

The awkward silence thawed somewhat with the arrival of the soup. The lady sitting opposite addressed me. She told me her name was Marie (she pronounced it 'Maari') Franklin. Her husband's name was Les and they were going home to New Zealand following a tour of Europe and the United Kingdom. In all they had visited nineteen countries, she told me proudly.

I liked her immediately for she seemed kind and genuinely interested in me. She was openly delighted when I explained I was going to live in Auckland. They were Aucklanders by birth and very proud of their city. Les Franklin was more reserved than Marie and instantly noticeable by his shock of thick white hair. He had a sailor's face, sunburned and crinkled, with a pair of keen dark eyes topped by shaggy brows. Marie sparkled and chatted with everyone but Les was a man of few words. Blessed with a wicked dry humour, I was soon to learn than when he spoke he was generally well worth listening to. He smoked a nautical-looking pipe and had a passion for boats and steam engines.

When the rest of the meal arrived, I realised I was really very hungry. I tucked into roast beef and all the trimmings, followed by lemon meringue. I had a second helping of desert and guiltily mourned the demise of another diet.

In addition to enjoying my meal, I fell in love. The steward in attendance on our table was one of the most gorgeous specimens of the Opposite Sex I had ever seen. Tall and slim-hipped, he moved around the tables like a panther. He had curly brown hair that lit up with auburn tints and a pair of dark eyes you could drown in. His features were classic Olympian Greek and I wickedly recalled a school visit to the British Museum. All those naughty statues with fig leaves over the interesting bits.

He chattered away to all of us in a barely comprehensible Anglo-Greek accent, but this didn't matter as he appeared not to expect a reply. His eyes smouldered at me every time I caught his glance. I flushed bright red and mused about Greek gods and goatskin-clad shepherd boys.

The next afternoon, the ship docked in Rotterdam. It was cold and unpromisingly overcast but I decided to go ashore to buy some chocolate and post cards. I went alone. Kerry hummed and haw'd so much about her wardrobe – should she wear the brown fun-fur or the grey one? – that I deserted her in disgust and made my own way out of the docks into the town.

Rotterdam turned out to be more attractive than I expected. There was a well laid-out shopping centre surrounded by narrow streets of tall houses. Many little bridges crossed the canals and pausing for a moment on one, I could make out the blue-and-white funnels of the *Ellinis* sandwiched between the cranes and derricks.

It must have been the lunchtime rush hour. It seemed the entire population was on the move, most of them on bicycles. This made walking quite hazardous, as they shot out from nowhere, in groups of no less than fifty at a time, and sped hell for leather along the cycle tracks.

I browsed around the shops and optimistically tried on a pair of yellow hot-pants. These were all the rage at the time and I longed for a pair. With an effort I squeezed into a size fourteen. The effect was not pretty although I had no doubt that the cabin crews would have been appreciative. Determined not to leave empty handed, I settled for a Marc Bolan tee-shirt and the latest copy of *Cosmopolitan* magazine.

I discovered a delightful little coffee shop built on a large traffic island in the middle of the main street. Choosing a table next to the window, I ordered a cappuccino and tried not to feel too embarrassed that the staff spoke such perfect English. Out of the window I caught sight of two pairs of familiar figures, one pair fat, one pair thin. May and Sarah closely shadowed by their respective other halves. Sarah, as usual, was holding forth, brandishing a guide book in one hand and pointing up the road. May was looking longingly across the road to my coffee shop. A dispute ensued. Finally they agreed to differ. Sarah and hubby went off in pursuit of whatever, while May with her husband – whose name was Jack – came into the café and thankfully sat down at a table across the room from mine. May ordered tea for two and a selection of cakes. I noticed that she kicked off her shoes under the table.

Upon returning to the ship, I walked straight into the cabin and found Kerry kissing Mike. She looked extremely pleased with herself and was what in novels might be described as in a state of *dishabille*. Actually she was wearing a silk pink kimono but in my opinion that was sufficiently *dishabille* for before six o'clock. There was a large love-bite on her neck.

From Mike's pained expression, I gathered he would have cheerfully thrown me overboard as sharkbait. I pretended I had seen nothing.

'You should have come with me,' I told her, flinching as Mike stormed out and slammed the door. 'It had to be better than hanging around here all afternoon.'

'That's all you know,' was the reply. She helped herself to my *Cosmopolitan* and fell inelegantly on to Sarah's bunk.

I grabbed a towel and headed for the showers. 'You might at least have locked the door,' I felt it incumbent on me to remark on the way out.

25th October 1973

Dear Kate (I wrote)

Hi! Just a few lines to let you know I'm having a great time. Thanks for your leaving present. The St Christopher earrings are lovely.

I've met lots of nice people, mostly New Zealanders, including one crazy girl who shares my cabin. There are hardly any unattached men about, at least none over sixteen or under sixty.

After Rotterdam we stopped in Bremerhaven for a few hours, which believe me was long enough. It was cold and horrible. When the ship docks it's quite funny to watch the British passengers. They have to rush to be ashore first, charging down the gangways with shopping bags and pushchairs. Then they spend their time ashore hunting for a decent loo or somewhere to have a cup of tea. Oh yes, and they complain about everything.

The prices in Germany are scandalous. I exchanged a couple of pounds into deutschmarks that bought me a postcard, one stamp and a bag of crisps. In the late afternoon, when all the new passengers had embarked, we left the last of the northern ports to head south – at last.

There was a lifeboat drill this morning. We had to put on our life jackets and report to Boat Stations. I got mine on back to front at first and had to be helped by one of the officers. Kerry – that's the girl in my cabin – took ages with hers in spite of having lots of help from the crew.

Guess what's on in the cinema today – *The Poseidon Adventure*. Can you believe it? I shall give that a miss. I'm afraid that today's boat drill has done little to reassure me about boats, and Greek boats in particular.

In a few days we shall be in Las Palmas. Hope it warms up soon. Write to me at Cape Town.

Wendy

CHAPTER IV

Kerry Goes Shopping in Las Palmas

SUNDAY MORNING dawned disappointingly grey and muggy in Las Palmas. The town was barely visible because of the sea mist, or perhaps its was urban smog; I wasn't sure which. Kerry and I left the ship together shortly after breakfast, taking packed lunches with us. The tourist bus at the docks was full so we walked the mile into the town. Kerry complained volubly about the distance but I closed my heart and ears to her and strode ahead.

Unlike me, she had no inhibitions about wearing hot pants. That day she had squeezed herself into a shocking pink pair with matching halter neck top. The identical nail varnish on her toe-nails completed the ensemble.

Kerry's blonde looks and bare legs attracted a great deal of attention on that walk. A white-helmeted traffic cop directing the cars from a little box in the middle of the road gazed transfixed as we passed, his whistle clamped firmly in his mouth like a dummy. Some boys on mopeds whooped their appreciation and tailed us along the road. I feigned not to notice.

Although it was late in the season, there were many holiday makers about. Because it was Sunday, there were very few shops open but we found a street market selling fruit and flowers, clothes and cheap souvenirs. A newspaper stand was doing a brisk trade to the English tourists buying out-of-date British papers. I stopped to buy one while Kerry vanished between the stalls without a word, to reappear a few moments later clutching a paper bag.

Then as now, nosiness is one of my greater failings.

'Well, what did you get?'

'Knickers,' I was tersely informed.

'I was only asking,' I replied wounded.

'I know you were and that's what I bought. Knickers. Two pairs. Okay?'

Recalling the bulging contents of her three suitcases, I stared hard at her for a second and suppressed the scathing comment that came to my lips.

We walked along a quiet narrow street which led to the sea. The sand, greyish and loose, was speckled with cans and litter. A group of young children played at sand-castles in front of a background of concrete apartment blocks and stark hotels. There were short, stunted palm trees everywhere, most of them bent down away from the prevailing wind. I jumped down onto the beach and landed almost up to my knees in loose sand.

Kerry pulled a face. 'I'm not bloody well sitting on *that*. It's foul.'

'Agreed. Look, there's some grass over there that doesn't look too bad. Did you bring a towel?'

'No way. I suppose you did?'

'Of course. I thought we might be able to go swimming.' I clambered up off the beach and shook the sand out of my sandals.

'Swimming! In that?' Kerry disdainfully indicated the torpid, slate-coloured water. 'You'll probably catch something. Swallow that water and you'll have the shits for a week.'

'Don't be ridiculous, it's not that bad. People pay good money to come here for holidays.'

'Rather them than me. Just wait until you get to New Zealand, then you'll see beaches. *Proper* beaches with surf.'

'Yes, I can imagine how you missed the surf in Cardiff,' I said nastily.

'Shut up and come over here. Now give me that towel and then I want you to put some of this on my back.' Kerry produced a large bottle of sun lotion from her bag. We both sat down on a strip of brown grass that consisted chiefly of bald patches of earth, but which was, at least marginally, cleaner than the sand. Kerry rolled over on to her front and undid the strap around her neck.

'Okay, ready, but mind you don't get it in my hair.'

'No, Ma'am.' I poured a sloshy dollop of the stuff between her shoulders and rubbed it all over, none too gently. When I had finished, I rubbed off the excess oil on to my own legs and announced, 'Now I'm going for my swim. Look after my watch please.'

A grunted assent. I slipped my dress off, as I was wearing a swimsuit underneath. Not for me the contortions of undressing under a towel. I stood up and ran down to the water and through the fronds of swirling seaweed. I took a deep breath and plunged in. It was balmy and gorgeous, and the view of the town was prettier from the water. To my left was a grey-stoned fortress called the Castillo de la Luz set in grounds of flowering shrubs – some variety of hibiscus, I thought.

As I floundered and splashed in the shallows, Marie and Les Franklin came into sight on the promenade and stopped to take photographs. I waved madly but they didn't see me. After a few more minutes I emerged from the water suddenly chilled, and went to find my towel.

Kerry was lying sound asleep on most of it. Heartlessly I rolled her over, reclaimed my property, and she flopped back into position again. I stretched out on the ground to dry in the sun and fished in my bag for a sandwich. I lay back down and tried to sleep but after fidgeting for about five minutes, I'd had enough. Kerry was still out for the count and I took care not to disturb her. I scrambled into my dress, which by then clung quite fetchingly to my damp swimsuit. I scribbled a suitable message on the back of an old envelope and attached it to Kerry's bag.

I was only just in time to catch the last bus excursion around the island for that day. I had to hurry to buy my ticket, then hopped on board to take the last remaining free seat. The journey was scheduled to take about two hours along the winding coast road and then turning inland through some of the most rugged and inhospitable scenery I had ever seen. We crossed the edge of the Maspolamas desert with its shifting dunes and stunted vegetation. In the far distance was a range of mountains called the Roque Nublo.

This was all an improvement on the disappointment of Las Palmas town. It was the first time I had ever seen real desert. I had been attracted to desert landscapes ever since, at the impressionable age of thirteen, on a wet Bank Holiday Monday, I went to the cinema to see *Lawrence of Arabia*. As a result, I developed an unhealthy desire to blow up a train while hiding behind a sand dune, read every book on Arabia I could lay my hands on, and, more happily, fell passionately in love with Omar Sharif.

The courier drew our attention to the soaring magnificence of the volcano called Teide and the bus stopped for a photo call. Some Japanese tourists sitting in the rear seat obediently leapt out in answer to the challenge. I kept to my seat and admired the view from there.

The bus continued along the mountain road and pulled off at an isolated roadside café. I enjoyed a cup of bitter, strong coffee and afterwards studied a rack of postcards until I found what I was looking for. It was a picture of Canary Island folk dancers, a swirling circle of red and white colours; the women in gaily tiered dresses and little flat black hats, the men in baggy, knee-length shorts and black sombreros.

I bought the postcard purely for nostalgia. Years before, at a Folk Festival in Sidmouth, the star attraction had been a troupe of dancers from the Canary Islands. They had clapped, sung and danced, bringing a welcome touch of exotica to that most reserved and English of resorts.

Back aboard the ship, the public rooms had been transformed into something out of the Arabian Nights. Many of the street vendors from the bazaar had been permitted on board to flog a dubious array of merchandise. The outcome of this shift from shore to ship appeared to have resulted in gross inflation.

I elbowed my way through the congestion and went below.

Kerry was alone in the cabin in bra and panties, dabbing awkwardly at her shoulders with a wad of cotton wool. I smelled calamine.

She looked daggers at me. 'There you are – at last! Just look at me, I've been eaten alive thanks to you going off like that. Bloody sandflies! Why the hell didn't you wake me up, I'd have gone with you?'

'I honestly didn't think coach excursions were your thing, and anyway I preferred to go by myself.'

She gave me a pitying look as though I had just confessed to some unmentionable form of deviant behaviour, but when I offered to do her back, she grudgingly thrust the bottle of calamine into my hands. Her fair skin was covered with a rash of angry red bites. I generously applied the soothing lotion to all and sundry.

'There, that should do.'

I went to take a shower. There were six tiny cubicles in all, in a room about ten foot square. The lighting was always inadequate, the atmosphere humid and stuffy. Without exception the floor was always awash with an inch or more of water. Sometimes the discharge outlet regurgitated a spout of brown muck. Whenever the ship was in port, as it was today, the showers emitted a malodorous smell.

I dived into the first cubicle and managed to drop firstly my towel and then my soap. I emerged a few minutes later having been alternately chilled to the marrow and scalded. On the way out I collided with May, who was coming in. She was enveloped in a huge quilted dressing gown and a matching shower cap.

'Oops! Sorry dear. Had a nice day?' In the confined space of the doorway we were obliged to cling together quite affectionately as each sidled past the other in her chosen direction.

Back in the cabin, Kerry had one of her prohibited suitcases open on the floor

She was kneeling down and sorting the contents into several neat little piles around her. It was this orderly jettisoning of items that caught my attention. In a long week of sharing living space with Kerry, I had grown accustomed to her rummaging through her belongings as though hunting for that elusive bargain at a jumble sale.

'May I ask what you are doing?'

'Having a sort out, dope. What does it look like?' she replied.

I examined the growing piles on the floor more closely. 'Kerry,' I began disbelieving, 'those are *all* pairs of . . . Kerry, for heaven's sake, exactly how many pairs of pants have you got?'

'Just these and those in the other bag over there.'

I sat down. 'I just don't believe this. There must be at least a hundred pairs there.' After a closer scrutiny I calculated this was an underestimate.

Kerry was unperturbed. 'I like them. You can't have too many and I like to match them up with whatever I'm wearing.'

By now she had completely emptied the case. She produced the paper bag containing that morning's purchase and added them lovingly to her hoard.

I reflected seriously on this as yet unsuspected trait in my new friend's character.

'My God,' I thought. 'I'm sharing quarters with a knicker fetishist!'

Piled up on the floor were just about every colour and style of intimate feminine apparel I had ever seen. Bikini briefs, satin French knickers, black lacy bits of nonsense, two-way stretch ones, some decorated with pretty pictures and some with vulgar anecdotes. And what was that one – my lord, it was a *thong*. From what I could tell, there was everything except regulation school navy-blue.

Having satisfied herself that all her treasures were present and correct, Kerry replaced the stockpile neatly into the suitcase, that then refused to shut. She sat down heavily on the lid to secure it – click, click – and shoved it away under one of the bunks.

That night at dinner I was the recipient of a note in the bread basket. This was a time-tested ritual between the dining room stewards and unattached female passengers. A note indicating a discreet rendezvous and the time would be found either under a plate, concealed in a napkin or, as in my case, slipped between a couple of bread rolls. Unfortunately my unknown admirer's attempts to arrange a romantic meeting were wasted as I read the note out aloud to the entire table.

It was signed 'Costas'. That was funny, I was under the impression that all Greeks were named either Nick or Mike. The writing was barely legible and scrawled on the reverse of yesterday's menu. From what I could decipher, I was invited to meet him on the Boat Deck, port side at . . .

I couldn't read any more so I passed the note to Marie Franklin for her opinion. She put on her glasses and held the paper to the light.

'*You come Boat Deck something, something*', she read. *'I give you very nice time.* I can't make out any more.'

'It hardly matters as I shan't be going. Boat Deck indeed! I wonder which one it is?'

I turned around and rudely stared at the room. Gosh, but there wasn't much to choose between them. There was the fat one staggering along under a pile of dirty plates. He was horrid and greasy and he winked knowingly at me. Or what about that one over there standing guard over the coffee pot? He kept staring in my direction. But he was so short. I didn't much care for short men. I was five foot eight and hated towering over smaller men, Latin types in particular.

The Adonis who served our table hovered behind me with a plate of veal cutlets and expertly served me a portion using two spoons. My heart did its usual somersault and I gazed up at him hopefully and received an impassive stare in return.

At the end of the meal I ritually tore the paper into small pieces and haughtily discarded them into the ash tray.

CHAPTER V

Crossing the Line

AT THE END OF THE first week of November, the *Ellinis* was nearing the Equator and at last I had the warm sunshine I craved. Leaving the air-conditioned comfort of the ship was like stepping into a wall of heat. From first thing every day the decks were strewn with bare bodies, the tanned ones and the fair, all soaking up the scorching sun rays like strips of bacon. I took cover in whatever little shade was available to keep my hated freckles in check, but even a limited exposure had done its worst. I was red, freckled and my hair felt like straw.

I didn't get to see very much of Kerry these days. I decided she only really needed me for shore excursions, when she was likely to get lost. She lazed most of the time in or around the pool, her fair complexion turning pinker by the hour. As was to be expected, my well-intentioned advice that it might be a good idea to cover up a little or do the tanning more gradually was met with the arrogant assurance that she of all people knew what she was doing, thank you very much. After all she was born and bred in New Zealand – God's own land where the sun always shone and so on. I took the hint and shut up.

The traditional Crossing the Line ceremony found everyone eagerly gathered around the swimming pool. Father Neptune, who incidentally bore an uncanny resemblance to Jon Denis, was resplendent in dark green tendrils, flowing beard and carrying a tinfoil trident. He was suitably attended by a bevy of sea nymphs, all with pieces of wet seaweed attached to their bikinis.

A proclamation was read out, buckets of water liberally thrown over the front row of spectators, and the event concluded with much horseplay in and out of the pool.

Late one particularly sweltering afternoon I went below and found Kerry prostrate on her bunk and complaining mightily about

Crossing the Line.

a devastating headache, nausea and other symptoms of sun stroke. Her back and shoulders were raw and May was fussing about with some liquid concoction that reeked of vinegar. Kerry yowled like a love-lorn tom cat and looked reproachfully at me as if this latest affliction was solely my fault.

May produced some large sheets of a sort of greaseproof paper, procured from one of the cabin staff apparently, and these she placed carefully in layers across her patient's sore back.

'There, that should do the trick,' she said. 'The paper will keep the oil from off the sheets. It's a very old remedy but it does work.'

'Thank you,' came a voice from the bed, none too gratefully, I thought.

After changing, I went along to the little cinema for the early programme. Today it was Malcolm McDowell in *The Raging Moon*, a moving story about the love affair between two paraplegics. Less than half way through, I was aware of a presence settling into the seat beside me. It was Kerry, miraculously recovered from her bout of sunstroke, with hair pinned up in rollers like a hedgehog and partially covered with a silk scarf.

The scarf I recognised. It was one a favourite auntie had given me for Christmas.

'That's *my* scarf you're wearing, you cow!' I accused her in a hoarse whisper.

'What was I supposed to do?' her retort came back. 'I couldn't find any of mine.'

She wriggled in her seat. Rustle, rustle. I tried to pretend I hadn't heard anything but two heads in front of us turned round.

'Kerry, have you still got that oily paper on?'

She giggled. 'Absolutely. It's inside my dress and I've stuffed it down inside me drawers.'

'I do not wish to know and for goodness sake, keep still!'

I began to lose all track of the film. Kerry crackled and rustled beside me. It sounded like someone opening up half a dozen packets of crisps and there was more turning of heads.

'Will you keep quiet!' I hissed.

A dark head behind us leaned forward and, in a voice of icy authority, sternly demanded that we either leave or be quiet. It was the Captain, godlike and omnipotent in mystic white-and-gold braided uniform. A chastened Kerry subsided into comparative silence for a full two minutes. Then I began to shake and the two of us, unable to restrain our laughter any longer, rose as one and left.

The rest of the row had no choice but to stand up and let us pass.

On the third attempt I wrote a letter to my parents.

10th November 1973

Yesterday, we visited Cape Town. I wish you could have seen it, it must be one of the most glorious cities on the world. It's very spacious with wide, open streets and expensive looking shops. There are houses and gardens built in terraces above the city and above it all is Table Mountain. Sadly, the mountain was hidden by low cloud yesterday. The locals call that 'the tablecloth'.

I went on a coach trip along the Atlantic coast road to the Cape of Good Hope. This road hugs the cliff-edge and the view is breathtaking. The sea was so clear it was possible to see the rocks and seaweed on the bottom.

The author near Cape Town.

There are long beaches and bays of silvery white sand. The houses are very smart and expensive, some modern, but best of all I liked the older houses built in traditional Dutch style. Everywhere there are spring flowers (remember, it's springtime here) and colourful rambling shrubs. Oh yes, I saw Christian Barnard's home, which is close to the hospital where the first heart transplants were done.

In marked contrast from the whites-only estates, are those set aside for the black people. Most of them live in shabby single-storey rented houses, but they are well cared for and brightly painted. The children stand barefoot on the dry earth and wave at the traffic.

The Cape Point Nature Reserve was disappointing. The only animals I saw were a tribe of baboons and some ostriches in the distance. The baboons came very close and played to the gallery to entertain the tourists, some carrying babies on their backs. The older males surged over the bus and hung upside down outside the windows. One particular old grand-daddy behaved quite obnoxiously – I will spare you the details – before swinging off to join his harem.

> There are two promontories at the tip of the African continent where the Atlantic and the Indian oceans meet – Cape Point and the Cape of Good Hope. This is where the legendary Flying Dutchman is supposed to sail. No-one visits Cape Point without hearing this famous ghost story or reading about it in guide books. The phantom vessel, which is alleged to sail for eternity off the Cape in an attempt to round it but never succeeding, is said to be the ship of a Captain Vanderdecken, who in the 17th century tried to round the Cape in a terrible gale. He swore that not even God would make him change his mind. For this blasphemy, so the tale goes, he was condemned to sail off the Cape coast in vile weather forever and to bring misfortune to all who sighted him. The curse would only be lifted should he find a woman who would be eternally true to him.
>
> The ghost ship can be distinguished from real vessels by the fact that she is wearing her full sails when others are unable to show an inch of canvas. There have been many sightings, including one by George V while serving as a midshipman on H.M.S. *Bacchante* in 1881.
>
> I regret there were no sightings by yours truly in 1973.
>
> I visited a craft centre and bought a carved Zulu warrior. There was also a tea shop serving English cream teas.
>
> Yes, I have received all your letters and I will write to the Kent cousins when I have time. Please send me newspaper cuttings of Princess Anne's wedding. Trust me to be on the high seas and miss it all!

I signed this letter with lavish affection and put it by to post in Perth.

The brief visit to Cape Town had left me feeling distinctly guilty because I'd enjoyed it so much. The spectre of apartheid was barely detectable. Everything had been so agreeable, the people pleasant and friendly, black and white going about their daily business, to all appearances oblivious of any racial discord. It was not until I had lived in New Zealand and observed at first hand the integration of the Maori and the Pakeha (white man) that the differences between that country and South African society became evident. As it was, I had a niggling feeling in the back of my mind that I had been duped in some way. I regretted buying the carved Zulu warrior now. Standing on a chest of drawers, it looked cheap and nasty and I re-wrapped it in a paper bag and put it away at the bottom of my suitcase.

It took a full week to cross the Indian Ocean from Cape Town to Western Australia. Fondly I had imagined it would be warm but in fact the *Ellinis* followed such an extreme southerly course that the weather became colder than I had ever known. The swimming pool was emptied and the sun decks all deserted. A few hardy souls, Les Franklin and I among them, turned out to pace the decks muffled deep in overcoats to combat the icy blasts from the south.

The sky, menacing and leaden, reflected upon a wild sea the colour of slate. Turning a corner into the wind was enough to force one to totter backwards against the force of the gale. The great ship pitched and tossed through the worst of it, some of the bigger waves even breaking over the lower decks. It was scary and exciting and I loved every moment of it.

Below, the corridors had been carefully roped up and sturdy paper bags placed at regular intervals. Some complained that the sight of these was enough to make anyone feel sick. The public rooms too were criss-crossed with ropes, which made dancing in the disco more interesting than usual.

I had started going to Greek dancing lessons every afternoon in the Ballroom. The music was provided by a well-worn tape, played over and over again on an old fashioned reel-to-reel tape recorder while the Entertainments Officer snapped and scolded. His class kicked and stomped away for a hour or so with more enthusiasm than aptitude, but to do *Zorba the Greek* when the floor beneath one's feet was listing first this way, then that, was no mean accomplishment. For those unlucky enough to be at the end of the line, it felt like hauling a train uphill.

I, who had been born with two left feet, suffered more than most from Jon Denis's bitchiness but the others laughed at him, not me, and wouldn't let me give up.

While the dancing went on, the rest of the Ballroom was transformed into a workshop, with rehearsals for *Annie Get Your Gun* at one end, groups of ladies industrially stitching away at costumes wherever they could find the space, and the Greek dancers high stepping it in between. Jon, God bless him, lorded it over all.

Marie Franklin and I had joined a daily debating group that met in the relative peace and quiet of the Outrigger Bar. This was organised by a self-appointed chairman who was a retired police inspector. He was utterly gorgeous, like a youthful Cary Grant, with smooth good looks and an indolent charm. He was causing some disapproval among the more stuffy passengers because of his undisguised interest in a young female passenger. Having seen the dimensions of his wife in profile, I was catty enough not to blame him. Still, I envied the young female passenger.

A dozen or so people regularly attended these debates and at the first meeting it was agreed – but not by me – that any topic could be put forward for discussion with the exception of Northern Ireland. Seeing that the Northern Irish problem was one of the most important issues of the decade, I considered this to be presumptuous and craven. All the old favourites were aired: the Pope and the Pill, the Common Market and Nuclear Disarmament. It was just like being back at school again and after four meetings I stopped going.

The rough weather continued. Sometimes the tips of icebergs could be seen and one bright morning, to the intense excitement of the handful or so on deck, a large whale surfaced not far from the portside of the ship. We all reached for our cameras and clicked away madly as the great mammal spouted water for us before submerging gracefully beneath the waves.

Late one afternoon the southern lights were clearly visible, shining above the polar cap. I asked Les how far away they were and he estimated about two and half thousand miles. I had expected to see the great colourful hanging curtain phenomenon, but all that was visible was a faint, shimmering glow. Even so it was a fantastic spectacle and all of a sudden I felt painfully homesick. 'My God, what am I doing here? I must be stark, staring bonkers.' Inexplicably I thought of my little dog. The poor thing would be wondering where on earth I'd gone. *Where on earth indeed?* I dashed in off the deck and scuttled into the first set of loos I came across. I locked myself in, bawled my head off for a few minutes, occasionally flushing the system to hide the noise. After that I felt much better and emerged in time to change for dinner.

That night there was a 'drag' ball, the ladies dressed as men and vice versa. In the subdued lighting it was hard to tell who exactly was who but the big give-away was where some of the 'ladies' were lopsided.

The nightly disco was always popular with the under twenty-fives. There was a live band on board called *The Mixtures*, an Australian group who had been at the top of the British pop charts with their record, *The Push Bike Song*. The band members were working their passage home with their wives and girlfriends and performed in the disco every night.

On the dance floor, owing to a dearth of men, the British girls danced away together or in groups. The Australian and New Zealand girls waited patiently to be asked by a man before they joined in. I explained to one Australian girl that in England it was considered quite normal for girls to dance together. She stared at me in bewilderment. I was pleased to notice that some of the Australian women were so staid and reserved that they made me appear almost extrovert. I found this to be most encouraging.

About this time there was a nasty bug going the rounds of the ship. It was quite usual for a virus of this type to get a hold in such confined living accommodation. Sarah and May caught it first and were really sick and they passed it to me. We sneezed and coughed miserably in chorus. Being the least incapacitated, I was sent to the ship's shop to purchase cough mixture and Beecham's powders. The powders tasted foul but May stood over me until I drank the lot.

Before we arrived in Western Australia, Kerry and I moved ourselves, bags and baggage, into better accommodation in some spare cabins, courtesy of steward Mike. Kerry went into a spacious four-berth cabin shared with some Dutch girls while I moved into a two-berth room at the opposite end of the ship. I was thrilled with the extra space but not so impressed in the early hours of the morning when the ship's engines, throbbing louder and louder somewhere at the back of my head, drove me into a nocturnal evacuation with a blanket to spend the remainder of the night curled up on a sofa in the Main Lounge.

As soon as the first bell went for breakfast, I collected my gear and returned, still dressed in a nightie, to my old quarters. Cramped they may have been but with Kerry gone, and if I could ignore Daisy's snoring, at least it was quiet.

CHAPTER VI

Perth, Melbourne and Sydney

MID-NOVEMBER and at last landfall in Australia. I was so excited, I scarcely slept the night before. The *Ellinis* docked overnight in Fremantle and we awoke to a golden day of brilliant sunshine and clear blue skies. I caught the bus from the shipping terminus into the city of Perth a couple of miles away. It was a pretty ride, past leafy gardens and smart bungalows, many with traditional brown tin roofs and all with shady, white verandas.

I had expected Perth to be a splendid city and I wasn't disappointed. The crowd on the bus eagerly dispersed into the shops, any of which would have rivalled Regent or Oxford Street's. I only saw one incongruous building, for set among the snazzy department stores and boutiques was a parade of mock Tudor shops complete with oak beams and jettied overhangs. They looked absurd in the scorching Australian summer sunshine.

What was really astonishing was the dazzling display of Christmas decorations strung across the streets. I had forgotten all about Christmas but here was a timely reminder in the eye-catching show of silver stars and tinsel that glistened and danced in the warm breeze.

I don't know whether it was the warmth or the festive spirit, but I felt enveloped in a delicious sensation of anticipation and well-being. I was here, on the other side of the world, gloomy England was thousands of miles away and I sparkled with confidence. Even queuing up for ages at the post office failed to quash my feelings and after I had posted off my letters and cards, I bought some sandwiches and spent the rest of the afternoon lazing in the park.

There were scenes of frantic activity and emotional leave-taking that day aboard the *Ellinis*, as many passengers had reached their destination in Western Australia. From Fremantle onwards, the ship

On board the ship en route to Melbourne.
Kerry (centre) with two other passengers.

was again designated as 'northbound', for people embarking here were heading for Europe.

The ship hugged the South Australian coastline for three more days of sun and relaxation en route to Melbourne.

Bright and early on the day the ship was due to dock in Port Melbourne, I resolutely paced the Boat Deck in order to clock up a mile or so before breakfast and on my second lap I noticed a strange man – strange as in unfamiliar, not peculiar – leaning over the ship's rail. Every time I rounded the deck, there he was. On the third lap, he turned slightly and smiled at me as I dashed past. He was fantastically good looking and I began to feel distinctly foolish. To my mixed relief and disappointment, the next time around he had gone. I trotted on, only to fall over a pair of legs protruding from a deckchair.

'Bloody hell!' I had all but landed in his lap.

'I was wondering what it would take to get you to stop,' came a voice with a warm Australian accent.

My cheeks flaming pink, I scrambled to my feet and mentally beseeched the deck to open up and swallow me. The deck remained firm beneath my feet. A pair of ice-blue Nordic eyes looked up at me. I wanted so very much to be somewhere – anywhere – else. Never had I felt so big and clumsy, or so horribly conscious of my windswept hair, which I should have washed the night before had not Kerry requisitioned my hair dryer for the whole evening.

I muttered 'Sorry!' and groaned. My God, how dynamically witty. Here I was being closely scrutinised by the Opposite Sex and I couldn't think of anything whatsoever to say. Luckily I didn't have to.

He stood up. 'Do you mind if I join you?'

I had the impression he was going to come with me whatever I said. He was in his early twenties, taller than I and slim. Dressed in jeans and a sort of open necked caftan thing, his hair was very fair and long, restrained by a coloured head band. My mother would never have approved, but I approved – oh yes, very much.

But old habits die hard and I replied lamely.

'Actually I'm in a bit of a hurry.' There's a lot to hurry for on a cruise ship after all. I started to walk away but as I had hoped, he fell into step beside me.

'I'm Jan-Yves,' he said.

I stopped in my tracks. 'Jan what?' I echoed rudely.

I should say he was accustomed to this sort of reaction and repeated with tolerant good humour.

'Jan-Yves. That's Jan Y-V-E-S. Got it? I'm Dutch.'

'You don't sound Dutch,' I said.

'That's because I come from Sydney. But originally I'm from Holland. I'm going to Holland now, to see family and have a long holiday.'

'I'm going to New Zealand,' I said flatly, while my heart sank. I recalled my day in Rotterdam four weeks earlier. It was twelve thousand miles from New Zealand to Holland, which is a very long way, but it would be another week before I left the ship in Auckland. On board ship, a week is a very long time.

As we walked, Jan-Yves explained that he was on vacation from art college, where he was studying design. His widowed mother had returned to Holland for a visit some time ago, re-married and settled there. He was planning to stay with her and his new stepfather for about three months.

We chatted together until the bell went for first sitting breakfast. Neither of us was in any hurry to leave but eventually Jan-Yves said casually, 'Well, be seeing you around, I expect.' He disappeared through the doorway leading to the stairs.

I remained where I was and stared thoughtfully for some minutes at the coast of Victoria on the horizon. The ship was due to arrive at Port Melbourne by mid-morning. Somewhere to the south lay Tasmania.

No, Mother, I concluded happily. Art student and apache head band. You would definitely *not* approve.

There was a regular suburban train connection between the port and Melbourne proper. With its dark red livery and well worn plaid seats, the train was like an antique version of the District line. It clunked and rattled the few miles from the docks into Flinders Street station, a main-line terminus that at one time could claim to be the busiest railway station in the world – or so my guide book informed me.

Melbourne was traditionally acknowledged to be an old-fashioned city. The elegant streets boasted restrained architecture of old-established stores and expensive boutiques, and the famous wrought iron balconies on some of the older houses were much in evidence. None of Perth's brash glitter here. Near the city centre was the spacious and lovely King's Park, resplendent with its colourful flowering borders and shady wooded paths. Here I wandered aimlessly for over an hour, mingling with the office girls enjoying their lunch break and young mothers with their children.

Adjacent to King's Park was the Melbourne Art Gallery, a stark, modern structure housing one of the largest art collections in the southern hemisphere, and it was here that I encountered Jan-Yves again. He was sitting on a low wall in the forecourt, busy sketching on a large drawing pad across his knees. His subject was a dark, metal-cast sculpture that might have been a female nude. The figure was impressive, about eight feet high with dimensions of breasts and hips to match. With its long features and unseeing eyes, it reminded me of the statues on Easter Island.

Jan-Yves' pencil flew over the paper in easy, confident strokes. The resultant image was warm and vibrant, without the cold, vacuous quality of the original. When he had completed the drawing to his satisfaction, he paused for a moment and then added a huge pair of spectacles to the lady's nose.

I burst out laughing. Jan-Yves tucked the sketch pad under his arm and we went together into the silky marble coolness of the gallery.

Like a great many other things, my arty phase had been inglorious and short-lived, but that afternoon my passive interest was rekindled like the phoenix rising from the ashes. Jan-Yves' quiet enthusiasm, his obvious knowledge of the subject, and his habit of suddenly looking at me intently as if I too was something worth looking at, had me enthralled. Still, I told myself sternly, he was probably only assessing my bone structure.

Following our tour of the art gallery, we took the bus on the short ride to St. Kilda. This was a popular suburban resort and we walked along the beach until we reached the quay where the *Ellinis* was berthed. She was flanked on either side by two battle-grey cruisers, each one bearing a hammer and sickle emblazoned on the bow. At the top of the passenger gangway, Kerry, who was chatting to some of the crew, swooped down on me. She stared curiously at Jan-Yves but I declined to introduce them.

'The mail's in,' she announced. 'I collected yours.' She thrust a couple of air mail envelopes into my hand. One was from my mother, the usual half a dozen pages of news plus a wadge of newspaper cuttings.

I made arrangements to see Jan-Yves again after dinner and hurried off to Marie Franklin's cabin.

I knocked on the door. 'Marie, it's me – Wendy. I've got some newspaper clips of Princess Anne's wedding. Do you want to see?'

Yes, she most certainly did. Marie was one of the most ardent Royalists I had ever met. During her stay in England, she had even managed to get inside Buckingham Palace and that had come about as follows. It is customary for visitors from the Commonwealth to sign in the visitor's book at their respective High Commissions, and so Marie duly put her name down at New Zealand House. She was fortunate to be selected to receive an invitation to attend one of the Royal garden parties.

In the meantime Marie, with her wonderful ability to make friends wherever she went, had become acquainted with a young New Zealand woman who was employed in Buckingham Palace as a maid. So when Marie triumphantly went off decked out in her garden party hat and frock, her new friend arranged for her to visit some of the rooms within the Palace itself.

Marie had commented, 'The carpets were quite threadbare in places actually.'

Nevertheless, the experience had been the highlight of her visit to the United Kingdom. Now we pored together over the creased, black and white pictures of an ethereal Princess Anne with her handsome new husband in the traditional balcony pose.

'They're coming to Auckland, did you know that? Marie informed me, 'All the Royal Family will be there in February for the Games. On *Britannia*.'

A couple days after departing from Melbourne, the *Ellinis* approached Sydney Harbour. It was early on Sunday evening and although still several miles distant, the famous skyline of this ocean city could be clearly seen. Behind the city was one of those spectacular sunsets that poets and artists dream about. A ball of red fire radiating bands of gold and orange, a blushing beacon that welcomed the great white ship to sail into its core of light.

All the decks were packed. I stood sandwiched between Les Franklin and a garrulous lady from Lancashire. Looking around for Jan-Yves, I eventually spotted him leaning against the rail on the flying bridge. Kerry was with him talking nineteen to the dozen. I was relieved to note that Jan-Yves was looking utterly bored.

The ship passed to the south of the notorious Sydney Heads. These are high cliffs where the local suicides make their leaps into the next world. Nosing into the Harbour was breathtaking, but at the same time it was all terribly familiar. On the left, the white wimples of the Opera House, then the tall Goldfields building, and, as all necks craned upwards, the famous bridge itself.

Kerry appeared at my side in a state of high dudgeon, because by now it was apparent that *Ellinis* would not be berthing at the more convenient Circular Quay but at the less accessible Pyrmont Harbour. If she didn't like the arrangement, I heatedly recommended she complain to the Captain. An unidentified male voice behind me echoed my sentiments.

'Ker-ist! What does she think this is? The bloody *Canberra*!'

It was fully dark when the ship finally dropped anchor, and all the time consuming disembarkation procedures were fulfilled. The Australian customs were very strict. One regulation was that no fruit might be taken ashore in order to prevent the spread of horticultural disease. All bags were thoroughly checked for smuggled apples and oranges.

Stern-eyed customs officials held audience in the ship's lounge. One nasty looking piece of work scrutinised my passport for a full five minutes and was most disappointed when he could find no discrepancy. He grudgingly applied the necessary stamp.

Kerry, having appropriated the first available taxi, was looking mightily pleased with herself.

'We're going up to the Cross,' she declared, snapping shut her powder compact and settling herself back into the seat. I peered out of the window to see better. I have often heard Sydney described as brash, but my impression on my first evening was of a mellowed city, at ease with itself, comfortably blending elegant Victoriana with contemporary glass and concrete. The shops in George Street were brightly illuminated, many with Christmas trees and coloured fairy lights. We drove past the famous square at Martin Place, dominated by the Gothic Post Office, and the Australia Square Building, which was the tallest in the southern hemisphere.

The square mile of King's Cross, Sydney's red light district, teemed with its ebullient and cosmopolitan community. Kerry and I left the taxi and strolled along the busy street, past bars and restaurants. Almost every European nationality was represented here. Most had tables set out on the pavement beneath gaily coloured umbrellas. Between the shops, inviting narrow streets led on to small, discreet squares overlooked by stylish colonial houses. Bright red creeping plants spilled from their tubs over the wrought-iron balconies.

The prostitutes, either singly or in pairs, paraded up and down their own little bits of territory. None of them appeared to be doing much business. Tourists were taking photographs of them, laughing and pointing. I noticed one very young girl in a black leather mini skirt and black tights. She looked like something out of a French farce but there was nothing farcical about the haunted, desperate look in her eyes. I really do hate men, I thought illogically.

Being possessed of a healthy curiosity about such matters, that night I visited a sex shop for the first time, with Kerry trailing reluctantly behind me.

An exquisite looking raven-haired Eurasian girl in a pink cat-suit perched on a stool behind the counter flicking through a magazine. There was only one other customer, a quietly dressed woman carrying a wire shopping basket, who appeared to be working her way through a shopping list. I nudged Kerry to look. I was shocked, impressed and hysterically amused all at the same time.

Most of the books on display were wrapped in polythene, which was a great pity, but there were one or two well-thumbed volumes of interesting photographic material available. I examined some of the gadgets for sale in a glass cabinet. I have a wild imagination but I could only hazard a guess as to their function.

'What's that thing supposed to do?' I enquired of my more worldly companion but as it turned out, Kerry was no better informed than I.

'Why don't you ask Miss Lotus Blossom?' she said.

'Honestly, Kerry, I'm not that fussed. Shall we go?' With my curiosity sated, we quitted the shop and I have never crossed the threshold of such an establishment from that day to this.

Our stay in Sydney was extended for two more days because all Greek shipping was being 'blacked' by the waterside workers and the scheduled departure was not possible. In order to catch up on some of the time lost, the authorities decided on a complicated course of action. All the hold luggage destined for New Zealand was to be removed from the *Ellinis* while in Sydney and held there for storage. It would then be reloaded onto the *Ellinis*'s sister ship the *Australis*, which was due to dock in Sydney about a week later. This meant that the *Ellinis* would remain in Auckland for only a brief three hours. All the hold luggage belonging to the unlucky passengers leaving the ship in New Zealand would not arrive until some time in mid-December, or whenever the good ship *Australis* put in an appearance. Needless to say this arrangement was greeted with a near-riot by passengers, but there was nothing else to be done.

It drizzled continuously for those two days. I explored Sydney extensively on foot, its museums, art galleries and, of course, the shops. A bus ride took me to Bondi Beach, which turned out to be nothing more than a wide strip of pale sand in an urban environment of tower blocks. There was no surf, or even a shark, to be seen.

One day Kerry and I lunched at the revolving restaurant at the top of the Australia Square Building. There was a special express lift just for the restaurant, ground floor to fiftieth in as many seconds. The food was indifferent but the amazing view compensated for it. Botany Bay to the south and the Harbour to the north, the heavy traffic on the bridge reduced to dinky toy scale.

The ship and its entire company were all thankful to depart Sydney on the Tuesday night. Jan-Yves had disappeared during our prolonged stay to visit friends living in Parramatta. He invited me to go with him but I got cold feet at the last minute and said no. I got the impression he was not very pleased with me, so I saw to it that we made up for precious time lost on the day that the ship belatedly arrived in Auckland.

I doubt that at the time I was really in love with Jan-Yves but I was very smitten with the idea of being in love, which was the next best thing. We made our farewells in classic style and it seemed only fitting that my arrival in my new country should be celebrated with the willing sacrifice of my detested virginity.

At any rate it whiled away an hour or so . . . and I did remember to lock the cabin door.

PART TWO

The Long White Cloud

CHAPTER VII

Auckland – Gift of the Sea

MY FIRST GLIMPSE of Auckland was on a muggy and very wet afternoon. The undemonstrative farewell at Southampton was more than made up for by the welcoming reception of New Zealand's Queen City. There were simply crowds of people gathered along the quayside or leaning over the visitor's gallery of the shipping terminus, calling out, waving and holding small children aloft, perhaps to be seen for the first time by visiting grandparents.

A Maori choir wearing traditional costume sang a song of welcome. At the other end of the quay a brass band oompha'd up and down. As the *Ellinis* was three days late, I couldn't help wondering if they had been at attention all that time, waiting and watching the peak-capped figure wielding the baton for the signal to strike up a tune.

Kerry was beside herself with excitement and jumped up and down yelling in my ear.

'Dad! DAD! Look there he is, over there.' She clutched at my arm and pointed at the mass of faces staring at us from the quayside.

It took a long time to disembark. I had already said most of my goodbyes but now May rushed up to me as I waited to go through customs. She bore a nautical look, arrayed in a white crimplene dress and a smart navy blue blazer with little anchors on the lapels. I was duly smothered in a hug and pecked on the cheek.

'Now don't forget,' she said breathlessly, 'we'll be returning home in the middle of May. You will come to see us off, won't you?'

I replied that of course I would and that I hoped they enjoyed their tour of New Zealand.

She patted my hand. 'Where's that nice young man of yours?'

She didn't miss much, didn't May. I said offhandedly, 'He's around somewhere . . .'

I was interrupted by a smartly turned out, fair-haired woman. 'Is this the last of your stuff, May? We may have to take a taxi after all. This won't all fit in the boot.' She smiled at me. 'Who's this?'

May introduced us. 'This is my husband's cousin, Eunice. She has lived in Auckland for many years.'

Jack's cousin Eunice had expertly gathered up most of May's bits and pieces in her arms and somehow managed to propel me along beside her.

'I'll give you our phone number, Wendy,' she was saying over her shoulder.

'You must come over for dinner. Frank will come and get you.' She paused long enough to fish in her bag for a pen and scribble something on a piece of paper which she handed to me.

'We'll look forward to seeing you. Don't forget, give me a call!' and she was gone. May was gone, Kerry was gone and I was left standing there like an abandoned waif.

A familiar voice growled in my ear. 'Are you going to stand here and take root, or would you like a lift?' It was Les Franklin, looking extremely pleased with himself. A very pretty girl with dark curly hair hung on to his arm. She was unmistakably a younger edition of Marie.

'Hello, Wendy,' she said, 'I'm Mariana. Welcome to Auckland.'

Les and Marie had three children. I had heard so much about them over the last few weeks that I almost felt that I knew them personally. Philip had just graduated from university, Richard was eighteen and the much-loved daughter, called Mariana after her mother, was a little older than me.

I gratefully accepted their offer of a lift. I had made a reservation to stay in a hotel for a week and it was here that the Franklins dropped me off. We went in two cars, Philip driving his father's and Mariana her own little volkswagen. Marie had very kindly invited me to stay with them for a few days but I had no wish to impose upon their family reunion so I stuck to my original plans. I had come away to be independent and some time I had to begin standing on my own two feet. All the same, I had accepted Marie's invitation to Sunday lunch.

The hotel was in Prince's Street, a wide, tree-lined avenue with many buildings connected to the university. I was shown to a pleasant, twin-bedded room with a telephone, T.V. and shower. Having had enough cold or boiling showers on the ship to last me a lifetime, I hurriedly asked if there was a bath.

There was no time to do any unpacking as I wanted to return to the harbour to watch the departure of the *Ellinis.* It was only a short walk from the hotel and when I reached the quay again, it was still packed with people, but I managed to recognise some familiar faces. It was dark by now and the ship was lit up like a Christmas tree from bow to stern. I eventually spotted Jan-Yves on the Boat Deck near the spot where we had first met – could it have been only a week and a half ago? I called out and amazingly he heard me and raised both arms above his head and waved. The Maori choir burst into song again and the ship slowly pulled away from the quay, imperceptibly at first until the gulf between Jan-Yves and me had widened to three ship lengths.

I watched and waited until the *Ellinis* was a shrinking cluster of white lights on the horizon. My last link with home had gone and taken Jan-Yves with it, for this was New Zealand and I was on my own.

It was strange to sleep in a proper bed again after six weeks in a narrow bunk, and for several nights my dreams were enhanced by the feeling of the slight swell of the high seas.

I hurried down to breakfast bright and early on my first morning and shared a table with two young Englishmen, also newly arrived the previous day, though they had come by air. They were from Basildon in Essex, which was only a few miles from where I lived. I was put in mind of Liza Minelli's song, *She travelled round the world to meet the guy next door.* Immediately after breakfast I ventured out into the sunshine to explore my new surroundings, armed with a street map provided by the hotel and a guide book.

I consulted the guide book first: *Auckland is the largest city in New Zealand. Built upon sixty-three volcanoes, it occupies a site between two magnificent harbours, the Waitemata and the Manukau.*

The name 'Waitemata' means sparkling water and now that last night's downpour had cleared up, Auckland was revealed as a spreading, modern city surrounded on three sides by this superb harbour. The largest of Auckland's volcanoes is Rangitoto, a conical

Rangitoto Island, Auckland Harbour.

and twin-peaked island out in the Hauraki Gulf. This famous landmark is visible from most of the city. It presents an identical face, no matter from what side it is viewed.

The Waitemata is spanned by the Auckland Harbour Bridge, which is only slightly less impressive than its counterpart in Sydney. This eight-lane freeway boasts two Japanese-constructed extensions on each side, referred to locally as the 'Nippon Clip-On', as Philip Franklin later informed me.

Although the Waitemata Harbour is a busy seaway, there is no disfiguring dockland to speak of. The water is constantly astir with pleasure craft, sailboats, hydrofoils, ferries and the occasional naval warship. From the lower end of Queen Street, great liners can often be seen at berth, to all appearances about to set sail up the city's main street. Auckland is a city that begins with the sea and ends with the sea. Its frontier is the ocean, the beaches and the surf. The land was first discovered by an ocean-travelling people, and this affinity with the sea is the legacy of all native New Zealanders.

Stand on a high hill in Auckland and you may comprehend more easily the love that these people have for their boats and their beaches. As far as the eye can see is water, islands and the lure of the distant horizon.

As this was a Saturday, the shops in the city centre were closed, for New Zealanders value their weekends. Friday night is designated for late-night shopping throughout the land and the only businesses open on Saturdays and Sundays are the corner shop dairies that sell everything from groceries and newspapers to milk-shakes and panti-hose.

I took a bus ride along Tamaki Drive to the beach at Mission Bay. Tamaki Drive is the coast road east out of the city and looks like a causeway, with open sea on one side and the land-locked Hobson Bay on the other. The road is well known for its rows of pohutakawa trees, the New Zealand Christmas tree, aptly named with its flame-coloured flowers, which bloom from early December onwards.

Mission Bay was a quiet and unspoilt place (at least I thought it quiet after the bustling razzmatazz of many English resorts), beloved of the sailing fraternity. In New Zealand this is a large percentage of the nation. There were boats everywhere: sailing dinghies bobbing merrily on the high tide and boats lying on their side on the beach awaiting transport by trailer. The original stone-built mission house from which the beach takes its name still stands in a small glade surrounded by tall Norfolk pines.

I sampled a milk-shake, New Zealand style. Firstly a large carton was filled almost to the brim with fresh milk and a dash of flavour added. As if this wasn't rich enough, two generous scoops of ice cream were whisked in until the mixture stood up in little peaks. The cost – about fifteen cents, and at least a thousand calories. I enjoyed mine very much and called it lunch.

The following day was Sunday. Philip and Mariana arrived to collect me for lunch. I was genuinely pleased to see them for, to be honest, I was missing my friends from the *Ellinis*. The Franklins lived in Remuera, one of the older suburbs of Auckland, which overlooked the inland water of Hobson Bay and beyond it, afforded a view of the squat shape of Rangitoto Island. It took only a few minutes by car and while Philip drove, Mariana chatted to me as if

From left to right, Philip, Les and Richard Franklin at the Savage Memorial, Auckland.

we were really old friends. She told me she was a kindergarten school teacher but presently between jobs. I liked her very much. After suffering Kerry's inconsequential nonsense for six weeks, it was a pleasant change to talk to someone who was doing something useful with her life.

Philip Franklin had recently obtained a second degree in engineering and was keenly looking out for a suitable post. He was quietly spoken like his father, with the same thick head of hair, though Philip's was very dark.

As the car drew up outside the house, Marie was standing on the front porch to greet us. She looked relaxed and very happy, as well she might after her much longed-for reunion with her family. I was enchanted with the house. It was a large bungalow, made of wood with a wide veranda and, typically, a tin roof.

'You should hear the racket when it rains,' Marie said.

The house was built on the side of a hill, so the back dropped away to a lower floor that accommodated the garage. This was something of a misnomer; most of the garage space was taken up with the family boat. The lounge was tastefully furnished but with a comfortable, lived-in look, and opened on to a patio that was the roof of the garage below. From here one enjoyed an uninterrupted view of the Harbour. The sight was still so new to me that I gasped.

I was introduced to the cat, Josh, a large and lordly ginger moggie who had just been soundly reprimanded for sitting on the roof of Les's newly polished car and leaving a trail of pussy footprints from the boot to the bonnet. The feline delinquent hid behind Marie's legs for protection and stared me out. Josh was very fond of his 'mum', who fed him, but not so keen on his 'dad', who thought a lot of his car and was, I gathered, likely to give him his pussy marching orders.

After lunch, Marie, Les and Philip took me out for a drive in the car. Firstly we went up to One Tree Hill and then to Mount Eden. These two are the highest viewing points in Auckland. Both volcanoes are extinct now, of course, and are laid out as parks. Mount Eden was once a fortified Maori *pa* or stronghold, and its grassy terraces could still be clearly seen. From here we had a lovely view of the Hauraki Gulf to the north and, to the distant south-west, of the Waitakere mountains over thirty miles away. It did not surprise me to learn that in area Auckland is the largest city in the world. It spreads out as far as the eye can see, sprawling and expansive as if its restless, sea-loving inhabitants have stretched out as far as they possibly could in all directions without actually getting their feet wet.

Crossing north across the Harbour Bridge, we came to popular Takapuna Beach, an inviting expanse of clean, wet sand. The ever-present Rangitito Island stood guard on the horizon. I kicked off my sandals and ran to meet the sea. It was very, very cold but I paddled until my feet went numb. Philip took some photographs of Les and Marie and me, and then we went to a beach café for tea.

Marie raised the subject of my finding a job. I pulled a face because I was having such a lovely time and I had no wish to come down to earth and think about work. I reassured her that I had some letters of recommendation from New Zealand banks in

London and that tomorrow, being Monday, I would start searching for a job in earnest.

The days when the New Zealand government had participated in the assisted passage scheme to increase the nation's tiny labour force were long since a thing of the past. However, there was still an unsatisfied demand for secretarial and clerical staff. Sipping my second cup of tea on Takapuna beach on a glorious afternoon, I was cheerfully optimistic.

The Franklins dropped me off at my hotel and there was a message for me at reception. It was a telephone number on the Tauranga exchange. In New Zealand local phone calls are free of charge but as this was long distance, I had to make a toll call through the operator.

Almost immediately Kerry's voice answered. 'Wendy? Where *have* you been? I called hours ago.'

Me: 'That's too bad. I went out for lunch with Marie and Les. How are you?'

Kerry: 'I'm fed up to the back teeth.'

Me: (exasperated) 'You've only been home for two days, for heaven's sake! And thank you, I'm fine too.'

She ignored my sarcasm and went on: 'I shall go stark, staring bonkers if I stay down here long. There's nothing to do and nobody to do it with so I thought of coming up to Auckland straight after Christmas. Actually I've had a great idea.'

I suspected that I knew what was coming and I was right.

Kerry: 'We could get a flat together, go halves on everything. Wendy, are you still there . . . ?'

Me: 'Yes, I'm still here.' *(You and me share a flat? Not on your life!')*

Kerry: 'Well?'

Me: 'I'll think about it. I was planning on flat-hunting tomorrow, number two priority after job hunting. Anyway, I thought you were going to do hotel receptionist work. Surely you'd live in?'

Kerry: 'I dunno. I haven't even thought about a job yet. There's nothing here. I suppose I could try the Intercontinental.'

The Intercontinental was the premier hotel in Auckland and directly across the road from where I was staying.

Me: 'I think that's an excellent idea, Kerry.'

I really didn't want to hurt her feelings but the thought of sharing permanent accommodation with Kerry, with her caprices, her PMT, not to mention her quirky collection of underwear, was just too much. I vacillated.

'I'll look into the flat situation and let you know. Okay?'

She rambled on for several more minutes about the misfortunes of living out in the sticks and then hung up.

A week later I wrote to Jan-Yves.

> So much has happened during the last few days that I don't know where to begin. Firstly I've found a job and, as you see, I've already moved out of the hotel and into a place of my own.
>
> I went along to the National Bank of New Zealand's main office in the city and they offered me a job straight away. They were so desperate I started there and then. This was the Auckland office. Next week I shall be moved to a branch in Avondale.
>
> I found this flat in the local paper and moved in yesterday. It's on the ground floor of a split-level house and was originally intended to be a huge play-room for the owners' children. Now it has been converted into an open-plan and self-contained unit. There's a garden too, with miniature orange trees growing and a lovely view of the city and the sea.
>
> I'm sharing it with two other girls, one English and the other a New Zealander. The English one is going back to the UK soon. Kerry has got some idea about moving in with me but I shall persuade her that it will be much too cramped, seeing the amount of gear she carries around with her.
>
> Everybody has been very friendly. I've seen the Franklins a couple of times and I went with a crowd from work to see the film of *Jesus Christ Superstar*. There was an office Christmas party to which I was asked too, even though I'd only been on the staff for four days. It doesn't seem a bit Christmassy to me, not with this hot weather.
>
> Some friends from England wrote to say things are really grim there at the moment, what with the three-day working and all the power cuts. It seems there will be petrol rationing too soon.
>
> I know that you gave me your address in Holland but I've lost it, so can you let me have it again. Write soon.

I took care to add my own new address and posted the letter airmail to Chandris Lines in Bilbao.

I had moved from the hotel into the flat on the previous day, and not a moment too soon. The gypsy life was starting to pall and I had been living out of suitcases for almost two months.

The flat, located in Mount Albert, was better than I'd hoped to find with my limited funds. There was a large living area with a kitchen partially screened off, two admittedly small bedrooms and a bathroom. It was equipped with the necessities of life, a television, telephone . . . and an electric oven. This item held no interest for me whatsoever. The art of cooking was one that both scared and mystified me and my mother's blackened and burnt cake tins bore the permanent scars of my activities in that direction. If I made a fruit cake, it inevitably ended up being eaten with custard as dessert. Juicy lamb chops underwent molecular reconstruction in the oven and emerged as sad incinerated remains that even defied the dog's digestion. No, as far as I was concerned, cooking was definitely out. I should live on salads and yoghurt and grow thin and interesting. My ambition was to face the world flat-chested and bra-less.

I arrived by taxi and the two girls came out to help me carry my things inside. Liz, the English one who was due to fly home in a few days, was small and bubbly. I followed her lead and she showed me my room. This was basically furnished with a bed, a large walk-in cupboard for clothes, and an old-fashioned dressing table. The window looked out on to the back garden and there was a pile of dresses and two empty suitcases on the floor.

Liz explained, 'I'm in the middle of packing but you can have this room now and I'll sleep on the sofa. It's only for a few days and for a couple of nights I'm staying with friends over on the North Shore. I'll get this stuff shifted out in a minute. Cuppa tea?'

The three of us sat in the living room, nursing mugs of too hot, strong tea. The other girl, Kathleen, didn't have much to say for herself. She hung on to Liz's every word and occasionally beamed at me from behind unflattering spectacles. She was fat and her tight jeans and un-ironed tee-shirt did nothing to improve her appearance. Unkindly I decided that she probably wasn't very bright, as she alternately scowled and grinned while her hand dipped absent-mindedly into the tin of biscuits at her side.

The author's flat in Mount Albert, Auckland.

Liz held court sitting cross-legged on a plump, orange beanbag.

'This is mine,' she said. 'I've no idea how I'm going to get it on to the plane.'

I didn't know either and I asked her why she was going back to England in the middle of winter.

She replied carelessly, 'Oh, I came out here a year ago to get married but things didn't work out so I decided to call it quits and head for home.'

In some ways she reminded me of Kerry. It seemed the world was full of young women embroiled in, or barely avoiding, matrimonial disasters. 'Have they never read Germaine Greer?' I thought angrily, 'Don't they yet know that there are other options?'

When we had finished our tea, Kathleen hauled herself out of her chair, brushed the biscuit crumbs off her lap on to the carpet, and offered, in her rather squeaky voice, to take me upstairs to the main house to meet the landlord. I followed her up a short flight of steps to an immaculately tiled patio and we waited at a side door.

Kathleen pressed a bell and stood back, her hands stuffed into the back pockets of her jeans.

The door was opened by a sweet-faced lady of about fifty who politely shook my hand and invited me in. Anne McCowan was in every way *genteel.* Originally from England, she had lived in Auckland for all of her married life.

'I come from Staines,' she informed me in her cultivated English accent. Her husband, Bob, was a great bear of a man, with thick bushy brows and the kind of black hair that never seems to go grey. He took my hand in a strong grip and bade me welcome.

As we talked, I sensed Kathleen fidgeting impatiently behind me.

'Kathleen will show you where the laundry room is, won't you Kathleen?' Anne McCowan was saying. 'You are free to use the washing machine any time at the weekend. But *do* remember to connect the outlet hose into the sink or it will flood. Kathleen will explain.' Her face paled as though recalling a painful experience.

In New Zealand it is usual for houses to have separate rooms for laundry purposes. The McCowans' utility room backed on to the kitchen and also had its own entrance from the patio. Kathleen gleefully related to me the story of the time when one of the tenants living downstairs had forgotten to put the outlet hose from the washing machine into the sink and as a consequence had flooded the kitchen, the lounge and halfway down the hall with foaming soapsuds.

'She,' Kathleen inclined her head in the direction of the house, 'nearly had hysterics. It took him the best part of an hour to calm her down. You should have heard the language – and her being so posh.'

I was following Kathleen back to the flat downstairs. She was giggling like a schoolgirl. 'She plays croquet. Croquet! I ask you! Off she goes on Ladies Day all dressed up in white like a bloody meringue, with a little straw hat on her head.' The girl squealed and hooted with laughter at this recollection while her bosom shifted ominously beneath her tee-shirt.

From that moment, I knew that Kathleen and I were never going to get on.

On my second Sunday in Auckland I visited Waiheke Island, an unspoilt holiday retreat out in the Hauraki Gulf. During my brief stay in the hotel I had become friendly with a man called John Svenson, who was Swedish and researched television documentaries. Having been overseas on an assignment, he had let his house but had returned a few weeks earlier than planned. Consequently he was temporarily living in the hotel. He definitely came under the category of being 'an older man'. He was intelligent and worldly and I was still daft enough to wonder what he saw in me. We went out for dinner one evening to a dimly lit and very intimate restaurant where the management knew him by name. There was a table for two, candles and a discreet waiter hovering in the background. Although I was not for one moment impressed with his well-practised technique, his gentle – and expensive – seduction, I did enjoy his company. He had a sharp wit and was keen to encourage me to talk about myself, which I have always enjoyed. Actually on that occasion I talked at great length about Jan-Yves.

Upon returning to the hotel in the small hours, when, not entirely unexpectedly, John tried to follow me into my room, I used some unladylike muscle and pushed him out. I was furious and shaken. However, he was not deterred by my unfriendly and ungrateful reaction, pleaded a truce and invited me to spend Sunday with him on Waiheke. By now I was under no illusions as to his motives but in the euphoric state of my first full week in Auckland, I wasn't about to turn him down. We arranged to meet at the Harbour at ten o'clock.

There was a regular ferry service to Waiheke, the largest of the islands in the Gulf and about twelve miles away from Auckland. John and I, however, took the seaplane, serviced by Mount Cook Airlines and known locally as 'One Thousand and One Rattling Rivets'. The flight took about ten minutes and then we were touching down in Waiheke's tiny harbour and coasting to the dockside.

I have only the vaguest recollections of that excursion. An ancient bus took us to the other side of the island to a beach called Onetungi, where we lunched *alfresco* at the one and only hotel. Afterwards we walked on the beach and it would have been perfect had I been with Jan-Yves.

When my date made his next pass at me behind a rock, I handled the situation in a really grown-up way and slapped his face. At first he looked amazed and then furious. He yelled at me to grow up, I wasn't a little girl any more. I yelled at him to go to hell and that I was going home.

The bus wasn't due for hours so I had no choice but to walk. It was nearly four miles but after I'd covered about half that hot, dusty distance, a couple in a passing car stopped to offer me a lift to the harbour. I thankfully accepted and caught the five o'clock ferry back to the city.

When I walked into the flat, the girls were washing up and I told them I'd had a lovely day. I took a shower, wrote my letter to Jan-Yves, then settled down to watch *The Onedin Line* on television.

Not surprisingly, I never saw John Svenson again.

CHAPTER VIII

Philip, Mariana and Richard

BEING EAGER TO CREATE a good first impression, on my first morning at the bank in Avondale I reported bright and early. As it was just over a mile from the flat in Mount Albert, I decided to walk. Kathleen gloomily predicted that I was sure to be late. She was wrong. I wasn't late but I did arrive hot, sticky and longing for a cold drink. The temperature in Auckland during December rarely falls short of 28 degrees, with a high humidity, only slightly relieved by the cooling breezes off the sea.

Avondale was a pleasant little place out in the western suburbs, its only claim to fame being its racecourse. The main street, the Great North Road, boasted a half-mile stretch of small shops with a covered walkway, a small wooden church, a primary school and a library. The bank was on one corner of the main cross-roads, a single-storey modern building, air-conditioned – but only just, and having far too much glass for comfort in the heat of summer.

I was ushered into a small glass cubicle bearing the legend 'B J Waterworth – Accountant'. I sat down and waited.

Brian John Waterworth, when he finally detached himself from his telephone to deal with me, turned out to be a deeply tanned, prematurely balding man of about thirty-six. Although he didn't have much hair, what he did have was brown and had a tendency to form little baby curls around the nape of his neck. He had very dark eyes and wished me 'G'day' in a lazy drawl. I decided that he fancied himself with the ladies and noticed he wore a thick gold wedding band.

While we talked, B.J. (I was never to hear him called anything else) clasped his hands behind his head and swivelled from side to side in his chair. Then, as if suddenly recalling where he was, he jumped up to escort me on my inaugural tour.

I was introduced firstly to the Manager, Mr Evans, a tall craggy

The bank in Avondale where the author worked.

man like a tree, with iron grey hair, and then to the rest of the staff, most of whom were too busy to do more than look up. B.J. showed me to my desk and I stared in disbelief and dismay at the typewriter. It was a large, cumbersome antique, liberally coated in snopake and desperately in need of a new ribbon.

He pointed to an open door leading to an overcrowded and disorderly stock room. 'You'll find everything you'll need in there,' he said.

That I sincerely doubted but at least it appeared that I was to be solely responsible for my own routine. I rummaged through the disarray of open boxes and files until I found some stationery, and eventually a spool of typewriter ribbon. This was in a box labelled 'Miscellaneous'.

When I emerged some minutes later, it was to find the banking hall totally deserted. Assuming they had all gone for their morning tea, I set to organising some of the disorder that came to light when I opened my desk drawers. Stuffed at the back of the lower drawer I discovered several old copies of *Playgirl* Magazine, complete with male nude centrefolds. These went straight in the bin – then I thought better of it and fished them out to take home.

A small girl with brown shoulder-length hair swinging Cleopatra fashion, and dressed in the dark green uniform smock that all female staff wore, appeared from somewhere at the back.

'Hi, I'm Geraldine,' she said. 'We're all out in the kitchen. We're having a shout. Come on out when you're ready.' She disappeared again.

I was left to muse on what she had said. *We're having a shout.* What was the girl talking about, I wondered, and assumed a shout must be some kind of acquired Maori tradition similar to the ritual *haka*, the famous warlike challenge when the warriors jump about and poke their tongues out at the Queen. I rather liked the idea. It was an original way to start the working week after all. First collect the mail, unlock the vaults – and then disappear out to the back to have a 'shout'. British bank clerks should take note.

I couldn't actually hear anything, so I decided to investigate. I found the door to the kitchen and peered in through a small inset window. Now that was funny. They were all there, sitting round the table stuffing their faces. I went in.

There was a warm chorus of 'Hello' and someone pulled out a chair for me. Set out on the table was a pyramid of cakes and doughnuts on a large plate. One of the girls pushed them towards me.

'No thanks, I'm on a . . . oh well, just this once.' I helped myself to a fat, cream cake. *I think I'm going to like working here.*

Geraldine explained. 'This is Jill; it's her birthday.' She indicated a clone of herself, long dark hair, green smock. (It was at least a fortnight before I could tell them apart.) 'It's her shout.'

Comprehension slowly dawned in my dull English brain. It was Jill's birthday and Jill had provided cakes. Jill was 'having a shout'. They might have said so in the first place. I helped myself to another cake and became resigned to doing without any spectacle of Maori war paint that day.

The remainder of the morning passed in agreeable confusion. Apart from myself, there were two other new recruits: Christine, a cocky sixteen year-old fresh from Avondale College, and a lanky youth called (and I couldn't imagine what his parents had been thinking of) Rudolph. If that boy could do anything wrong, he did it, and mostly before his first morning was out. By the afternoon he was merely repeating himself. Christine showed off her newly-acquired skills with the adding machines while Rudolph was eventually set to sharpening pencils.

I didn't do too wonderfully either. I was plugged into a dictaphone machine while I protested that I could do shorthand at 120 words a minute. Nobody was interested. Indeed, B.J. looked faintly alarmed that this Amazonian Pom he had been saddled with expected him to go through a 'take a letter Miss Smith' routine.

'Jocelyn never did shorthand,' he mumbled.

'Jocelyn never did a lot of things by the state of her desk,' I muttered under my breath and put on the earphones. The tape had been recorded by the Bank Manager for his diary and I could barely decipher a word he was saying. He had a very strong accent and together with the fact that most of the places he referred to were unfamiliar – and unpronounceable – Maori names, I was hopelessly lost.

Geraldine helped out a bit, then with constant reference to a map of Auckland – after all how should I know how to spell *Papatoetoe*? – I was able to make most of it up.

During the afternoon Mr Evans rumbled at me over the internal telephone: 'Put the billy on, there's a good girl.' I was learning fast. A 'billy' was a kettle and I was to make his tea.

The day finished with a hectic scramble from four o'clock onwards to balance the daily figures, a seemingly impossible task by the look of the ever increasing cork-screw of ticker tape that the adding machines were spewing out on to the floor. B.J. presided benignly over the proceedings with the calm assurance that '*she'll be right*', the New Zealander's stoical response to almost any crisis.

I left them to it, departed promptly at five and caught the bus home.

The next day I telephoned May's friend Eunice, the lady I had met upon my arrival. At first she couldn't remember who I was;

then, when she did, she insisted that I come for dinner that very evening.

'Frank will come and get you,' she assured me.

Frank duly appeared at the appointed hour, a kindly and soft-spoken man who escorted me out to his ancient car with an old-fashioned courtesy that made me feel like a promenade queen on her first date. He settled himself into the seat beside me, carefully adjusted his safety belt, double-checked mine, and then crunched the car into gear and drove like a maniac all the way to his home at One Tree Hill. We screeched to a standstill, the tyres scraping against the edge of the kerb. My chauffeur appeared not to notice and walked around the back of the car to open the door for me.

I found the house to be quite extraordinary, as it was built high up on piles. A flight of open wooden stairs led up to a wide balcony which completely encircled the place, giving it the look of a grounded house boat. Eunice leaned over the balcony dressed in a cream pyjama suit. She had a wine glass in her hand which she waved at me.

'Hello there! Come on up, dinner won't be long.'

I ran up the stairs and she greeted me warmly with a hug. 'It is *nice* to see you again,' she said.

A sliding glass door opened into a large open-plan lounge. In the centre was a huge stone fireplace; the grate was laid with logs and the mantelpiece decorated with horse brasses and Toby jugs. There was no carpet but the wooden floor was polished to a sheen, and set off the simple pieces of antique furniture to best advantage. It was all very rustic and charming. The kitchen was as small and compact as a ship's galley and had an excellent view of the summit of One Tree Hill and the memorial obelisk to the Maori people.

Eunice poured me a drink and said, 'We've heard from May and Jack. They're staying with some people down in Wanganui. There's a postcard somewhere.' She sorted through a stack of papers and magazines. 'Yes, here it is. Come on, bring your drink in the other room.'

During the meal, I learned that Eunice worked in the fashion department of one of the large stores in Queen Street. She looked several years younger than her husband and I was surprised to learn that she had a married daughter. It soon became obvious that this precious daughter's husband was not Eunice's favourite person. In fact, in her opinion he was wanting in all respects and she complained about him at length. She was eager to show me her daughter's old bedroom, which was like a shrine to the child she had once been. The bed was festooned with dolls and a cuddly doggie night-dress case lay on the pretty patchwork quilt. Everything was pink and white, the curtains, lampshade and carpet.

I'd had a room just like it once, soft and feminine and hated. At the age of twelve I replaced *The Light of the World* with a poster of The Walker Brothers and painted two walls navy blue. I wondered if my own mother would exhibit such sentimentality about the boxes of books and pop-art posters I had left behind.

Eunice missed England very much. She spoke nostalgically of her home in Northamptonshire and of the little house they had lived in for a few months when first married. Frank had joined the New Zealand police force and they had come out here to fulfil a dream of life in the sun. They had a beautiful home and a holiday cottage up in the Bay of Islands, but Eunice still hankered after a terraced house in Wellingborough and popping into Marks and Spencer.

We sat talking until it was very late and then, when Frank took me home, Eunice came too. I had the strong impression that she wanted to see for herself that I was comfortably settled. They dropped me off at the side drive and it wasn't until I had let myself in and closed the door that I heard the car move off.

Bob and Anne McCowan took Kathleen and me to the airport to see Liz off at the end of the week. Her flight was delayed so we sat in the bar for most of the evening. Some of Liz's friends turned up to say goodbye and Bob crammed about six of us on to a seat and took a photograph.

As anticipated, the large orange beanbag proved a problem. Liz boldly marched up to the check-in counter with it clutched under one arm, but as her two bulging suitcases were already way over the weight allowance, it was obvious that the beanbag would have to be left behind.

She thrust it at me. 'Here, you'd better have it. You look a beanbag sort of person.'

'Why Liz, that's about the nicest thing anyone has ever said to me! I shall be sure to take great care of it.'

Her flight was called eventually and we all trooped out to the viewing gallery to watch the plane take off. It was a gorgeous evening with a perfect turquoise sky and very still.

In the car going home, Mrs McCowan reflected at length on what a *nice* pleasant girl Liz had been. Sitting in the back, I stuffed the beanbag on the floor between my feet and Kathleen munched noisily on a bag of crisps.

There was a lot more space in the flat after Liz's departure, but I was impatiently awaiting the arrival of the *Australis* so that I could reclaim my cabin trunk and the rest of my luggage. In the meantime I thought it prudent to work on attaining some level of compatibility with Kathleen. I didn't see very much of her as she left early for her job in the city, usually before I was up. She went to bed ridiculously early and during the time that we were together, she was either eating or had her nose buried in the voluminous edition of the evening paper. This she read avidly from cover to cover, spreading the discarded sheets all over the floor.

One of the hotels in Queen Street held Friday night discos and I suggested that we should go. Firstly she protested she would miss her favourite television programme, secondly that she didn't have anything suitable to wear, and then finally came the truth. She never went to discos.

I shrugged and said 'Okay, fine. I don't mind going on my own.'

A few minutes later she flounced into her bedroom, to reappear half an hour later made up to the nines and wearing a black mini-dress and platform sandals.

'I'm ready,' she shrilled.

I was beginning to learn that Kathleen's reactions to the unexpected followed a pattern: first mistrust every suggestion, say 'no' to everything – then think better of it afterwards.

The evening was not a great success. I should say something about the social habits of young New Zealanders, whose entrenched interests lie in the great outdoors. Sailing, canoeing, hiking, rock climbing and sport. All these are high on the list of popular recreations. Pubs, clubs and dances are not. In any case, pubs were never very desirable places to visit and were patronised almost exclusively by men. The licensing hours were short and the bars all closed at ten o'clock, when the clientèle came staggering out. The Maoris were always well and truly plastered and it was normal to have to step over their supine bodies as they lay where they fell, propped up against the shop fronts in Queen Street.

Auckland possessed many excellent facilities for outdoor sports, about ten cinemas in the city area alone, and an ice-skating rink. There was, however, only one discotheque, which was the one that Kathleen and I found ourselves herded into. It was like being squeezed in a trouser press.

It was in a low-ceilinged basement, plushly carpeted, with an area of bare floor in the middle of the room that could scarcely have been more than ten feet by ten. On to this were crammed over a hundred people. Naturally the women outnumbered the men by three to one. The sexes adhered strictly to their designated zones, men clustered at the bar, women clustered around the tables.

I cupped my hands and yelled above the racket into Kathleen's ear: 'I think you were right about discos. Is it always this crowded?'

Her reply was inaudible so I elbowed my way to the bar and queued up for ages to buy drinks at hotel prices. We stayed for an hour and then, in agreement for once, fought our way out.

On the Saturday before Christmas, the *Australis* was due to dock in Auckland, so in the late afternoon Marie and Les Franklin and myself, together with Philip to act as porter and chauffeur, and Mariana who came along for the ride, arrived together at the harbour to claim our late luggage.

Not entirely unexpectedly, the *Australis* was delayed. The quayside heaved with people and I soon spotted several *Ellinis* veterans intent on the same mission as ourselves. The brass band and the Maori choir were also in attendance. It looked as if it was going to be a long wait.

While I was getting coffee from the vending machine in the visitors' lounge, I looked out of the window and spotted Kerry getting out of a car in the street below. The driver, whom I assumed to be her father, took the car further along the road to find somewhere to park. Kerry looked sun-tanned and gorgeous and she greeted me effusively like a long-lost sister. We found a couple of seats and I told her all about my flat and my job in Avondale.

Kerry said, 'I've got an interview at the Intercontinental in the New Year. Will it be all right if I stay with you for a few days?'

'Yes of course, if you don't mind the sofa.'

'Quite honestly I don't have any choice,' she replied peevishly. 'I'm skint. I tried to get a temporary job in Tauranga but there wasn't anything and my Dad won't give me any more money.'

'Gosh, that's tough.' I was able to say, straight-faced.

She looked at me archly. 'By the way, did you ever hear from that Australian?'

'You mean Jan-Yves? Yes, I had a letter from him a couple of days ago, from Curacao. And he's not Australian, he's Dutch.'

'Huh, you could have fooled me! He's an Aussie through and through.'

I knew full well that Kerry had not liked Jan-Yves, mainly because he had not paid her enough attention.

'Did you ever hear from Mike?' I asked in a voice like syrup.

It was well on into the evening before the *Australis* finally berthed and the off-loading procedures began. It was mayhem. Passengers were coming and going, and irate *Ellinis* people were all searching for their property. While no one was looking, Mariana and I slipped up a service gangway under the noses of the crew. The *Australis* was much, much bigger than the *Ellinis* but not nearly so nice, I thought.

It was fortunate that we went on board because stacked in a corner were about a dozen or so trunks together with some suitcases and crates, all clearly labelled '*Ellinis*'. My trunk was among them and the Franklin's luggage as well. Mariana and I hurried ashore and triumphantly reported our find.

We loaded the car. Philip drove his parents and sister home and then brought me back to Mount Albert. We carried the trunk in between us, and then I made some coffee. Philip admired the flat but he had only one comment to make about Mount Albert in general, that it had too many churches and not a single pub.

When he had gone, I spent the next hour unpacking. Most of the things I pulled out now seemed ludicrous and impractical, with the exception of my mother's duvet and some winter clothes. There were my favourite books and a few records, and some old photograph albums. I flicked idly through them, family snaps in the main and some horrid ones of myself riding a fat Thelwell type pony with my hair in plaits. There was a loose picture at the back, a photo of my friend Kate and me on holiday in Yugoslavia. We were standing in front of the grey pile of a Roman amphitheatre in skirts up to our bottoms.

I went to bed well after midnight with my well-read copy of *Cider with Rosie*. Curled up cosily under the duvet, I browsed through the first few pages and succeeded in removing myself mentally to far-off Gloucestershire. Then I slept.

The festive season was upon us, although I couldn't get used to the idea of Christmas trees and seasonal celebrations in such gloriously warm weather. Belatedly I tackled some Christmas shopping, the second time around for me that year, as I had chosen presents for family and friends in England before I left. Marie had invited me to lunch on Christmas day, so I bought small gifts for the family and a couple of bottles of wine to take with me.

Kathleen had departed for her home town in Kawerau a hundred miles away, and the McCowans invited me upstairs one evening. I really didn't want to go but not wishing to appear rude, I duly accepted. There is an extended holiday in New Zealand over Christmas and the New Year and for the schools it is their long summer vacation. Anne and Bob had their two grandchildren staying; the elder was a little mentally handicapped girl who needed to be carried around everywhere, but her grandmother coped with this burden with much courage and joy. The younger child, a boy of four years, was adopted. He was part Maori and his bronze tinted skin and solemn dark eyes were evidence of his Polynesian blood. He may have looked like an angel but he was always in trouble of some sort, as Anne reported wearily.

Philip Franklin invited me to an end-of-term party at the university college where he had just graduated. Everyone congratulated him warmly on his success as he had just been accepted for a post with a French oil company in Kuwait. He was planning to leave for Europe in February to spend some training time in Paris, and then make a short trip to England.

Though Philip was the kindest of men, I don't think I enjoyed that party very much. I was out of my depth intellectually. Everyone appeared to be a science graduate and they all had a great deal to say for themselves. I consoled myself with the thought that at least I had a job, whereas most of them didn't. With its high standard of education and small population, New Zealand always produced a large batch of graduates in the science, engineering and medical fields – but surplus to home requirements. As a consequence, most of them had to seek employment overseas.

I was pleased for Philip but I knew I would miss his friendship and good-humoured teasing very much. Like many an only child, I longed to be part of a large family and the younger Franklins had quickly fulfilled the roles of the siblings I had always wanted.

To my disappointment, Christmas Day began cool and drizzly, so there weren't many turkey dinners taken down to the beach that day. It really was too bad! Had I come all this way for a chilly, grey Christmas?

I wasn't exactly in a penitent frame of mind but I made the effort and went to church. Philip's observation about the abundance of houses of worship in the Mount Albert area had not been exaggerated, for there was one on almost every corner. Mormons, Methodists, non-Conformists and Born Again Baptists, all these had their ugly brick-built temples, usually surmounted with a gilded cross pointing the way to Heaven and bedecked with floodlights.

Being conveniently Church of England, I had no qualms about sampling any that took my fancy. In the misspent days of my early teens, I had tried them all – and that included brief attendance at a North London mosque and a Buddhist temple.

I elected to go to the Baptist church that day because it was nearest. The service was very up-to-date and enthusiastic; everyone sang much too loudly and at one point several individuals stood up to enlighten the rest of the congregation as to how they had been saved.

'Jesus will save *you*!' they exclaimed fervently.

Not just yet, I hoped just as fervently. It always made me feel exceedingly uncomfortable when people talked about the Lord as though he were liable to drop by in person at any minute. Far, far

The Franklins' home in Remuera, Auckland.

preferable is the dignified tranquillity of an old Norman church, all whitewashed pillars and stained glass, and an uninspiring sermon from the pulpit that permits the mind to wander where it will.

I put a generous donation in the collection plate and made my escape.

The bus took me to Remuera and I walked into the Franklins' kitchen to find Marie disappearing head first into the oven to baste the turkey, or *chook*, as poultry is called in New Zealand. It is considered something of a luxury; the meat most frequently consumed is mutton or 'hogget' and, not surprisingly, lamb, which is reserved for export.

There was an enormous decorated Christmas tree taking up one whole corner of the dining room, where we gathered an hour later for dinner. Les carved the bird and we all sat round hungry and expectant with knives and forks poised when, with a little shriek, Marie suddenly remembered her beautiful home-made stuffing, still sitting in the oven.

Christmas Day 1973.

The traditional meal was all the more appreciated because of the unseasonably cool weather. Hot weather or not, Richard the younger boy enjoyed his food to the extent that his appetite was something of a family joke. He ably tackled a plate twice as large as anyone else's and still found room for whatever else was going. Mariana, on the other hand, picked at her food like a sparrow until her mother worried that she would fade away before their eyes. Inevitably Richard happily disposed of anything his sister left. He was a strikingly handsome boy, something of a loner and most certainly a rebel. I warmed to him because of this, but disappointingly, he was mostly unaware of my existence.

Richard's ambition was to be accepted at medical school to train as a doctor and he was working hard for his final examinations at school. He was definitely going through an anti-everything phase that left Marie in despair. During her first week home, she had undertaken the mammoth task of clearing out Richard's bedroom. This normally resembled the set of a disaster movie, not to mention the gruesome collection of bones and worse sitting on the dressing table. She had found some simply dreadful old rags mouldering under the bed and in righteous disgust dropped them straight into the bin. When Richard came home from school, there was hell to pay over the loss of his favourite clothes.

'The others were never like this,' Marie mourned to me privately and was frankly astonished when I confided that I thought her *enfant terrible* absolutely gorgeous – rags, tatters, bare feet and all.

Mariana had found a temporary job at a garage and car-rental agency down near the Harbour. Her parents were not in favour of this but Mariana was quietly determined to do her own thing. I never fully understood why she had given up her work at the kindergarten when she was so dedicated to little children, but it was to be some months before she resumed teaching again. She never enjoyed robust health but the garage work appeared to suit her friendly temperament exactly.

In the New Year, the Franklins were off to Waiheke Island for a three-week holiday down at their 'batch'. Going down to the 'batch' was a national institution. The term is derived from the 'bachelor' homes that young single men frequently built for themselves, and most families enjoyed summer visits to their holiday cabins at some idyllic coastal retreat.

I also planned a short break over the New Year. An old friend and her new husband, who had emigrated to New Zealand about a year before, had invited me to visit them over the holiday. Elaine and Michael Farrow lived at Lake Taupo, the vast lake in the centre of the North Island.

On Boxing Day the rain obligingly cleared up so I took a picnic lunch down to Mission Bay and spent the day lazing in the sun. In the evening I phoned my parents in England. It was the first time we had spoken since October, but even so there didn't seem to be much to say. I gabbled on and on about how fantastic everything was but they seemed confused and kept repeating how clear the line was; somewhere in the background I could hear the television and the dog barking.

After I'd hung up, I felt detached and alienated as though I'd been conversing with complete strangers. I went to sit outside in the garden for a while and watched the friendly lights of the city twinkling below me. Strains of music floated through an open window from the McCowans' television and I heard Bob's deep booming laugh. It was still and humid and, when large drops of rain began to fall, I went back inside to pack a few things to take with me to Taupo.

CHAPTER IX

New Year at Lake Taupo

EARLY ONE EVENING before the New Year Elaine and Michael drove up to Auckland to fetch me and we started out on the return trip to Taupo just before midnight. It was a journey of nearly two hundred miles and would take about four hours. We had completed about half this distance when the car stalled and refused to start again. We were just beyond Roturua, the town best known for its geysers and hot springs. It was a lonely stretch of road that cut through a pine forest, menacing and primeval. There was nothing else for it but to get out and push.

Actually the exercise was welcome, for although it was midsummer, it was bitterly cold. There was still some snow capping the mountains and the sharpness of the air took one's breath away. And the silence! The silence was like a living thing, something black, velvet and forbidden.

Michael and I applied motive power from the rear while Elaine took the wheel. Fortunately the road inclined in our favour, a narrow shaft of silver between the dark rows of sentinel trees. In the moonlight, it was almost as bright as day. After a few protesting hiccups, the car's engine coughed into life again. Michael and I jumped aboard quickly before it could change its mind.

We stopped briefly once more a few miles short of our destination at a viewing point overlooking the lake and watched the short summer night erupt into a spectacular pink sunrise. Lake Taupo is the largest lake in New Zealand, some twenty miles long and seventeen miles across. It reminded me of a Scottish loch. Ringed by mountains, the tree-line stretched almost to the water's edge, leaving only a narrow strip of charcoal-tinted sand. Numerous bays and inlets have made the lake a popular tourist resort, but in recent years it has also emerged in importance as part of the hydro-electric scheme centred on the town of Turangi on its southernmost shore.

During the summers of '73 and '74, with the country enjoying an unprecedented period of dry, hot weather, constant checks were kept on the water level in Lake Taupo. This was necessary to maintain the heavy demand for electricity supplies to the surrounding areas and the heavily populated region of Auckland.

When we reached the lakeside, it was almost daybreak.

Michael was a carpenter currently employed on the construction of a huge motel complex along the shore, and he and Elaine lived in a modest motel unit about a mile outside of Taupo. I hadn't seen them since their wedding for they had left for New Zealand immediately after their honeymoon, together with Michael's children from his first marriage.

I was interested to see how Elaine was coping as step-mother to a pair of seven and ten year-olds. She was younger than I and had married Michael without parental approval, for she had known him only for a few months before agreeing to start a new life in New Zealand and take on a ready-made family as well. To judge from initial appearances, the change had done her good. They both looked well and happy and Taupo was certainly a beautiful place in which to live, but I imagined it could be deadly dull in winter.

Their motel accommodation was a compact apartment with one twin-bedded room where the children slept, a tiny kitchen, bathroom and a living room where Elaine and Michael slept on a put-you-up. I had brought a sleeping bag with me, generously lent by Kathleen, who had been quite indecently pleased to see the back of me for a few days.

The two little girls, Kirsty and Caroline, were still sound asleep when we arrived. (The lady in the unit next door had been looking after them.) Elaine was cheerfully unconcerned one way or the other, and after putting on the kettle for tea, she set about seeing to the needs of her animals, an Alsatian bitch a few months old and a new kitten. There was a small puddle on the kitchen floor courtesy of the dog, who fell about in paroxysms of ecstasy at her mistress's return and then turned her affections on me. I adore dogs of any shape or size and Elaine's daft hound and I romped around on the floor to express our mutual approval of each other.

Elaine grabbed the animal by the collar, hauled her over to the back door and pushed her out. The dog rolled over and over in the heavy dewy grass, all four gangling legs waving in the air, before shaking herself heartily and loping towards a small copse of trees, pink tongue hanging out and mouth grinning.

It was too late now to bother about getting any sleep, although Michael, who had driven most of the double journey, dozed in an armchair, his mug of tea still held precariously in one hand. Elaine and I, who had never been short of a word or two, rapidly made up for a year's separation, with me imparting the gossip from home as to who was going out with whom, who was engaged and who wasn't.

The children appeared from their room shortly before seven o'clock, rubbing the sleep from their eyes. When they could focus, they stared at me bemused.

'You remember Wendy, don't you?' Elaine said, unwrapping a loaf of bread and popping two slices in the toaster. Obviously they didn't remember me at all. I tried to pretend that I liked children, which I didn't – dogs yes, children no – and smiled encouragingly.

'Hi Kirsty,' I said to the bigger of the two.

'I'm not Kirsty; *she's* Kirsty!' retorted Madam Caroline, and sat down at the table with one leg folded under her.

Elaine bustled about making breakfast. 'There's no more cereal, I'm afraid. It'll have to be toast.' She ordered Caroline to sit up properly, let the dog in, who was scraping madly at the door, and lit another cigarette. 'I'll have to go to the shops this morning, then we can have an early lunch and go out somewhere this afternoon.' She looked at me. 'You all right? You look as if you're going to drop off at any moment.'

My eyes were heavy and I felt light-headed from lack of sleep. 'I'm okay,' I lied. 'Any more tea?'

The small town of Taupo was totally dedicated to tourism. It was built round a pretty little harbour where pleasure craft bobbed at anchor and regular sight-seeing cruises were advertised along the wooden jetty. The streets were wide and lined with trees; all the shops looked new, with some very expensive boutiques, gift shops stocked with tacky Maori souvenirs and others selling mainly nautical gear.

Elaine completed her shopping at the supermarket and then we stowed the bags in the car and walked along the lakeside path until we reached the Taupo Lookout. This viewing-point over the lake is reached through an ornately carved Maori gateway. I bought some ice creams and we sat among the tourists admiring the view; the dark lake and the three peaks of Mount Ruapehu, Mount Ngauruhoe and Mount Tongariro on the other side of the water.

Lunch was freshly baked bread, cheese and salad. Afterwards we set off again in the car. Caroline refused to come with us, preferring to stay at home with her transistor radio for company. Elaine insisted on driving as she had not yet passed her test and wanted to have as much practice as possible. I noticed, though, over the next few days, that she wasn't shy of discarding her 'L' plates and setting off alone when the notion took her.

Our first stop was at the Wairaki Falls, a magnificent system of waterfalls gushing into a gorge of luxuriant native bush. A short drive away from Wairaki was the thermal centre at Orakei-Korako – the locals pronounce it 'Araki-Kraki'. This was on the other side of the great Waikato River and reached by jet boat. Orakei-Korako is well known for its multi-coloured silica terraces. Michael explained that the constantly changing colours are caused by hot algae springs. Great jets of steam spurt out from the terraces and spew up little fountains of boiling, coffee-coloured mud.

All this thermal energy is put to good practical use for the benefit of the local people. Many homes in Taupo are entirely heated by the underground springs. In their back gardens can be seen narrow metal tubes inserted into the ground and spouting hot, gurgling steam. In the Maori homelands around Rotorua to the north, the Maoris still take advantage of this ever-present source of cheap energy on their doorstep for cooking purposes. A joint of meat, carefully wrapped in a specially designed container and left in a steam hole in the garden first thing in the morning, will be thoroughly and succulently ready for dinner that evening.

It was a short walk from the springs to the sacred Maori cave called Ruatapu. In fact this cave was a vast tunnel entrance disappearing beneath a sharp overhanging cliff of silica rocks coloured in subtle golds and browns. Its floor was submerged under a shallow, tepid pool that could only be reached by scrambling over a steep scree of loose stones and boulders. Elaine refused to make the descent because she was wearing high-heeled sandals, but Kirsty, Michael and I slithered down, our voices echoing off the cavern roof that rose almost a hundred feet above our heads.

The walls ran with rivulets of water that plopped loudly into the pool and on to the rocks, gradually wearing away fissures and staining them dark green. I stood Kirsty on one of the rocks to take a photograph. She posed for me happily with the aplomb of her seven years, one hand on her hip, the other behind her head, and pouting.

It was chilly down there in the cave and I wasn't sorry when we made our way back into the afternoon sunshine to find Elaine leaning back against a warm rock with her eyes closed. Michael tucked her hand through his arm as we strolled back to the car.

Back at the motel, after we had eaten our evening meal, thirty-six hours without sleep finally caught up with one and all even though it was barely nine-thirty. Elaine flaked out on the sofa and I took my sleeping bag into the children's room and laid it on the floor between the two beds. I crawled in, closed my eyes and slept the clock round.

Next day was New Year's Eve and a barbecue on the beach was planned for the evening. In the afternoon I took the two girls with me for a trip out on Lake Taupo in one of the pleasure launches. Away from the shore, the water was surprisingly choppy. Dark threatening rainclouds had blown up from the south-west obscuring the mountains, but when we returned to the harbour in Taupo, the town was still basking in warm sunshine. In spite of the uncertainty of the weather, the barbecue went ahead as planned as soon as it was fully dark. It was a communal, neighbourly affair held on the motel's private beach, and about four families attended.

Barbecues are a way of life in New Zealand, encouraged by the suitable climate and the average Kiwi's desire to get himself out into the great outdoors. The habit is catching. On any weekend afternoon during the long summer months, wisps of black smoke may be seen rising from behind fences and hedges like Indian smoke signals as a thousand and one steaks are ritually sacrificed.

As New Year parties go, that one on a lakeside beach on a balmy night under southern skies had to be one of the best. Many of us went swimming, some unencumbered with bathing suits – after all it was dark. The real pleasure of swimming in Lake Taupo at night is in finding one of the many currents of hot water flowing from the underground springs and then floating in it.

The beach too had its hot spots. In colour it was very dark and speckled with quartz. It was most pleasant to bury one's feet in the loose sand to find a nice warming patch.

After midnight the storm that had been threatening all day broke. Heavy stinging raindrops fell down and there was a mad scramble to gather up the remaining food, the cooler boxes and the beer. Elaine's silly dog ran excitedly around in circles getting in everyone's way and then yelped when I accidentally trod on her foot.

The party reconvened indoors. I don't remember when it ended or when I went to bed, but when I got up in the morning there were still several sleeping bodies sprawled cosily together on the floor.

The dog had made another puddle in the kitchen.

That day I was due to return to Auckland, but we were all so tired that we sat for a couple of hours contemplating each other over the rim of our coffee mugs. I was the first to pull myself together and started to tackle some of last night's washing up. Michael disappeared to check the oil in his car. No sooner had the door closed behind him than Elaine took me completely by surprise and burst into tears.

'I hate it here, I really *hate* it! I want to go home,' she wailed between heart-rending sobs.

I had been on the receiving end of Elaine's morning-after lamentations before but on this occasion I conceded that she probably had good reason. I fished in my bag for a clean tissue and passed it to her. 'Come on, blow hard. And again. Now what's the matter?'

She sniffed inelegantly and little streams of mascara ran down her cheeks.

'Oh you've no *idea* what it's been like,' she began. 'Do you know, when we got off the plane in Auckland we were more or less broke. One day I had to go shopping to get some food with no more than two dollars in my purse. Michael could only find unskilled temporary jobs, and at New Zealand House they had made it all sound so easy. Then the offer of this job in Taupo came up and we took it but there's *nothing* here. I swear that if I have to look at another mountain, I'll go crazy.'

'Then talk to Michael about it. *Tell* him how you feel.'

'What's the point? He reckons it's all so bloody marvellous. He's got his job and his mates while I stay at home and play at keeping house. And there isn't even any real housework to do in a place this size.' She looked around her surroundings with loathing.

'Then get a job! Even a part-time one would be better than moping here and you could do it while the girls are in school. And I do think you should discuss things more with Michael. He might be as homesick as you and thinks that *you're* the one enjoying it.'

She looked at me doubtfully. 'You really think so?'

'Quite honestly I don't know what to think but it's a possibility and you ought to tackle him about it. If you're fed up with looking at pretty views, then come and stay with me. Any weekend or, better still, Kathleen's going on holiday for most of February and you could come then. We can go shopping or see a film. There's even a disco in Auckland and though it's not exactly the Ilford Palais, it's better than nothing.'

My friend's natural buoyancy was starting to reassert itself. 'Could we fix a date now?'

'The first weekend in February. Give me a call a couple of days before and I'll meet you at the bus station. Now I suggest you run along and fix your face!'

I said goodbye to Caroline, who was still hugging her transistor, and to Kirsty, who was quite sweet really. Then we set off for Auckland late in the morning. We stopped for a quick lunch in Rotorua but there wasn't enough time to have a proper look round or visit the geysers at the Maori village of Whakarewarewa. In the Maori language a 'wh' is pronounced as an 'f'. The aforementioned place is usually shortened to *Whaka* and is pronounced as *Foka*, which really doesn't sound very nice at all.

I took over the driving from Rotorua onwards to give Michael a break. He curled up as best he could on the back seat and was soon sound asleep. Elaine, true to form, talked non-stop next to me all the way into Auckland. Soon after leaving the motorway, we were in Mount Albert again; I nosed the car into the drive alongside the McCowans' Ford. Elaine roused Michael and we all three climbed stiffly out. I was home.

The front door stood wide open and the sound of voices drifted out. More precisely it was one voice, and one that I knew only too well. I dumped my bag inside the doorway and peered around the bamboo screen into the kitchen.

'What are *you* doing here, may I ask?'

It was Kerry, standing at the draining board and grating a large lump of cheese over a plate of lettuce.

Hardly bothering to look up, she said: 'Oh there you are at last. You might have told me you were going away. I came up yesterday to spend the New Year with you. Where's the chopping board?'

'Under the sink.' This unexpected picture of a domesticated Kerry was one I hadn't seen before and I started to laugh. She glowered at me indignantly and went on, now giving her attention to dicing up white cabbage.

'You know, you really are the limit because I did tell you I'd be coming up after Christmas. I've got that interview at the hotel tomorrow.' She produced a green pepper from a bag and sliced into it with feeling. 'So seeing that you weren't around – honestly, for somebody who's only been in the place for five minutes, you know more people that I do – Kathleen and I went out on the town. Didn't we, Kathleen? Now what's so funny?'

'Nothing!' I choked, trying very hard not to think about what an unlikely pair Kerry and Kathleen would have made doing the night-spots of Queen Street. Kathleen, still in regulation jeans and tee-shirt, nodded happily in recollection. Belatedly I remembered Elaine and Michael still hovering behind me. When I had done the introductions, Kerry virtually ordered us to sit down and eat as there was plenty to go round.

I did as I was told. If Kerry wanted to play hostess, I was more than happy to let her. Elaine and Michael appeared slightly bemused by my irrepressible new friend, while Kathleen ogled at her with the undisguised heroine worship I hadn't seen her display since Liz had left.

Kerry addressed me. 'There was a call for you from Mrs Franklin. She seemed quite surprised to hear me. Something about Waiheke on Sunday.' She passed around the tea cups. 'Oh, there's a letter for you too. From Holland.'

'Where is it?' I asked menacingly.

'I put it on your dressing table but it'll keep. Drink your tea.'

I was inclined to agree. I had no desire to read a letter from Jan-Yves with an audience, so I curbed my impatience and concentrated on doing justice to Kerry's nice salad.

We all waved goodbye to Elaine and Michael when they left to return home to Taupo, then I took my precious letter out into the garden and sat in my favourite spot by the little orange tree. Jan-Yves had written quite a bit, mainly about his family and their home in Amersfoort. The best part came at the end. He had written:

I shall come and see you in Auckland on my way back to Sydney in a couple of months. If you want me to.

He's coming back to me. Jan-Yves is coming here. I permitted myself the luxury of a little romantic speculation, then carefully folded up the letter and stuffed it in my pocket.

That night I did the decent thing and let Kerry sleep in my bed, which she had occupied anyway the previous night. I resigned myself to yet another night on the floor in the sleeping bag.

'Kerry,' I said when she had finished her nightly routine of putting in rollers and slapping on face cream, 'I'm really quite pleased you're here.'

'Liar!' was the grunted response.

'Idiot. I meant *here* in Auckland. I do hope you get that job.'

'So do I,' she yawned. 'By the way, I couldn't help noticing last night. You don't half read some funny books.'

'Eh?'

'I mean, just who the hell is Laurie Lee when she's at home?'

CHAPTER X

Waiheke Island

I DIDN'T HAVE TO GO into work the next day so I accompanied Kerry into town for her appointment at the hotel. The Intercontinental was Auckland's newest and most prestigious. It was situated, as I said before, in Prince's Street, almost directly opposite to the small hotel where I stayed on my arrival in November.

Her interview was for eleven o'clock, so I arranged to be back in time to meet her for lunch. I watched her disappear through the revolving doors looking trim and immaculate in a dark dress and jacket. Having time to kill, I made my way down to Queen Street and along to one of my favourite places, the Cook Street market. This was in an old warehouse and was run by hippies. Here it was possible to buy anything from handmade pottery, ethnic headgear, joss-sticks and – what appealed most to me – the cheapest range of clothes in Auckland. I liked to wear long, hand-made dresses in natural fabrics and I always bought them in Cook Street market. The price of clothes in New Zealand was very high compared to London and I saved a fortune by shopping at the stalls.

The hippie is a resilient species. When threatened with extinction at the end of the Flower Power movement in the late sixties, many had migrated from their natural Californian habitat west across the Pacific to find sanctuary in the islands of New Zealand. In 1974, I'm glad to say, the hippie was alive and well and living in Auckland, still bedecked with beads and granny-specs – and holding love-ins among the shady glades of Albert Park.

That morning I treated myself to some pretty scented candles, lazily sold to me by a bare-chested, cross-legged guru, who then promptly retreated back into his transcendental narcosis. Yeah, man, yeah.

I returned to the hotel to find Kerry. She was waiting for me in reception and it was apparent from the look on her face that she had good news.

'I'm starting next week,' she told me. 'I'll have a room here as well. Let's get a bite to eat, then I'll have to get back to Tauranga this afternoon. I'll hitch a lift'

'Hitch a lift?' I muttered disapprovingly. 'If you're that hard-up, I can give you the bus fare if you like.'

'You can treat me to lunch instead. Oh, don't be silly! This is New Zealand, not Britain. Everybody hitches. I bet you I can get a lift in five minutes.'

'As long as that!' I said.

We had a salad roll and coffee, then returned to Mount Albert for Kerry to collect her things. Only one suitcase and a shoulder bag this time, as she was travelling light.

I watched her set off confidently along the road in the direction of the motorway. 'I'll be seeing you next week some time,' she called and had gone barely a hundred yards when a passing car slowed down and then stopped. I watched her exchange a few words with the male driver and get in the car. She waved her hand at me through the open window and was gone.

During my short absence over the New Year, Marie Franklin had phoned and left a message inviting me to spend the next Sunday down at the 'batch' on Waiheke.

Unlike my previous visit, this time I caught the ferry, an ungainly double-decked little vessel that appeared seaworthy – but only just. The boat turned out to be more diverting than the sea plane, due to its fascinating cargo of passengers. Camping families and hikers, guitar-strumming hippies, grandmas and grandpas and lots of Islanders. This was the collective term for the Polynesian people from Fiji, Samoa and the Solomons. They filled the boat in their brightly coloured gaudy clothes and battered old straw hats. Then there was the Milk, the Meat, the Bread and the Mail.

There was as much to watch off the boat as on it. The sailing fraternity was out in full strength that bright fresh morning; bronzed and bearded men in little towelling 'pork pie' hats and skimpily clad girls who waved to the ferry as it passed. There was the Royal Yacht *Britannia* in dock at the Devonport Naval Base for a refit before the Commonwealth Games. Further out in the Hauraki Gulf were many small islands, grassed but treeless, and inhabited solely by grazing sheep.

In Waiheke harbour, the ferry drew alongside the jetty for the passengers to disembark. Most piled on to the little fleet of ancient buses still doing faithful service and hurtling wildly around the Island's narrow, twisting lanes.

Once again my final destination was the beach at Onetungi and so was everyone else's, to judge from the look of the crowd pouring on to the bus. It was standing-room only but I was grateful to find a place at all, and hung on for dear life as the vehicle roller-coasted across the hills to the other side of the Island. At Onetungi, the bus jolted to a sudden stop about a foot from the beach to disgorge its passengers, all of whom, with the exception of myself, disappeared from sight like rabbits into burrows. They would not be seen again until it was time to go home.

For want of something better to do, I flopped down on the sand to soak up the view. Onetungi is like the edge of the world. A track of a road runs for a couple of hundred yards in each direction until it gives up the effort as not worth while and dwindles into a footpath. On one side of the road is the wide, white sandy beach lapped by the calm blue water of the Gulf. Beyond the Gulf lies the Pacific Ocean. Lush grasslands dive steeply towards the beach in narrow terraces that provide a precarious foundation for the colony of wooden chalets and bungalows clustered there. Very few buildings were on level ground, just the hotel where I had lunched with John Svenson and some older wooden houses with white verandas. The post office and general store stood almost on the beach and enjoyed an unchallenged commercial monopoly.

Of human inhabitants there was no sign until two familiar figures approached me from the narrow cliff path. Les and Philip Franklin, unmistakably father and son, one white-haired and the other dark.

I stood up and was roughly grabbed from behind by something wet and cold and bodily lifted up off my feet.

'Do lay off, Richard,' my assailant's elder brother remarked conversationally, 'Put her down.'

No, don't put me down, Richard. If you want to play Tarzan with me, then that's absolutely fine! Regrettably, 'Tarzan' decided he had had enough and that it must be time for lunch. He led me up the cliff path, still dripping wet from his swim, a towel draped around his neck.

The Franklin's 'batch' nestled on a crow's nest perch in a small sheltered hollow. It was a comfortable, weather-beaten cabin and at present filled to overflowing with some cousins of Marie's who were visiting from Christchurch. A small tent pitched a short distance away was where Philip and Richard slept. Mariana reclined on a sun-lounger in white shorts and a bikini top, most of her face hidden behind a huge pair of sun glasses.

There were too many of us to eat inside, so the dining table was carried out on to the grass and we all fitted around as best we could on an assortment of chairs. Everyone talked at once as usual; Marie asked if I had enjoyed my visit to Taupo and one of the Christchurch cousins insisted that I *must* call on them if I went down to the South Island. Les wanted to know when Richard was going to take his turn and do some work on the boat while Mariana was saying something about getting an HGV licence so that she would be able to drive the supply truck for her hiking club. Philip grinned at me across the table and I smiled back, relaxed and utterly happy. Britain was on another planet and nothing else existed except for a remote island where a family of warm-hearted New Zealanders and an English stranger enjoyed Sunday lunch in the warm Antipodean summer sunshine.

After the meal, Marie and Mariana took me for a walk over the cliffs. It was hard work, uphill most of the way, and I should like to be able to say that I was merely out of condition. But the shameful truth was that I had never been *in* condition. I was accustomed to walking the dog for his constitutional around the block on a Sunday afternoon before settling down to watch the film matinee. I was ill-prepared for a cross-country trek on a hot day. The other two looked set to go for miles but Britain's honour was at stake, so I said nothing and toiled grimly after them.

In due course we came to a treacherously steep path down to the beach. It was just as long a walk back but at least it was on the level and we paddled most of the way. For me the attraction of a New

Zealand beach was its emptiness. Admittedly Onetungi is isolated even by New Zealand standards, but the overcrowded resorts of Europe, where the sand is covered by regiments of deckchairs and umbrellas, is thankfully unknown in this country.

Back at the 'batch', there was just time for me to have a quick swim and then I had to catch the bus to the ferry. The sound of the bus's old engine could be heard grinding down the hill long before the bus itself could be seen. The grandmas, the holiday makers and the hippies all appeared on cue and scrambled aboard. I waved goodbye to the Franklin clan standing in a group outside the general store as the bus moved off, only to halt again a few yards along the road to wait for a late passenger making a last-minute dash and hampered by the surf board under his arm.

At the harbour, a fiery evening sun hung like a red ball just above the sea as, with engines throbbing noisily, the little ferry eased its way out from the jetty to head west towards Auckland.

CHAPTER XI

A Royal Visit to Auckland

IT WAS NOW NEARLY the end of February and three months since my arrival in New Zealand. My new surroundings had become loved and familiar and if I ever suffered a twinge of home-sickness, I was too proud and too pig-headed to let on to anybody.

Kerry, now working full time and living at the Hotel Continental, was in her element. She wore a smart black dress to work and piled her hair up in a black velvet bow. She also had acquired a good looking boyfriend called Ross. With the boyfriend came a sailing boat, a sports car and an apartment in St Helier, which was the 'in' place to live for those lucky enough to afford it.

I met Ross only a couple of times and we disliked one another on sight. He may have been good in bed, as Kerry claimed, and impressive on the quarter deck (or vice versa), but I considered him loud, chauvinist and boring. In turn he thought I was weird and stuck up. I knew this for a fact because I overheard them talking about me. Kerry showed some unexpected loyalty by saying that I was all right once you got to know me even if I did have a posh British accent and talked as if I'd swallowed a dictionary.

When they had gone, I felt quite unreasonably jealous and binged for the rest of the evening on some of Kathleen's biscuits.

One weekend late in January I went to Rotorua on what was meant to be a coach excursion, but as only five people had booked seats on it, the travel company laid on a large black limousine instead. The big car ate up the hundred and fifty miles to Rotorua with ease and attracted much attention in the towns it passed through as pedestrians and motorists alike peered curiously to see who we were. Of the other passengers, two were Australian and two a young couple from Hertfordshire in England.

The first stop was at Ohinimutu, an ancient Maori village on the shore of Lake Rotorua. Here can be found one of the most unusual churches in the world. St Faith's is an Anglican church built in the classic English style, complete with tower and steeple, but it is made entirely of wood and heavily carved and ornamented in the Maori tradition. Inside, behind the simple altar, is a dramatic stained glass window. It is a representation of Christ walking on the water. The figure is wearing Maori costume and because the surrounding glass is clear and the window directly overlooks the choppy waters of Lake Rotorua, it appears to an observer within the church that the image is really walking across moving water.

I lingered for so long in this church that I was nearly left behind when it was time to leave for the Maori village at Whakarewarewa. This is well known for its geysers, boiling mud pools and, when the wind is blowing in the wrong direction, the pungent stink of bad eggs. Access to the village is through a carved wooden gateway that leads into a palisaded replica of a fortified *pa*. This one is called Rotowhio and here our small party was met by one of the famous *whaka* guides. These guides are all women and are always known by their first names; many of them have been decorated by the Queen for services to Maori culture.

The Rotorua Thermal Reserve comes under the control of the Maori Arts and Crafts Institute and is financed entirely by revenue from tourism. The Institute's aim is to promote Maori art in a wholly practical way, with the training of young men and women in the traditional skills of weaving and carving, and to re-establish the crafts of the Maori people, which otherwise would be lost.

The main attractions, of course, are the geysers. The most spectacular one is the Pohuto geyser, which spurts clouds of hot steam upwards to a height of sixty feet or more. It 'plays' intermittently for periods ranging from twenty minutes to several hours. Best of all, I liked the mud pools caused by heated gases escaping through the mud from subterranean caverns. These form into fascinating plopping bubbles and concentric rings, rather like mud-coloured porridge.

The paths around these pools are very well marked, and with good reason. The guide, with some relish I thought, related the gruesome story of a know-it-all American tourist who, armed with his camera, ignored the warning signs and stepped aside to investigate one of the mud tarns. He lost his footing because the ground was soft and gave way, and the unfortunate man disappeared into a hole where the temperature ranges from 250 to 350 degrees centigrade, and with a depth reputed to go straight into the earth's crust. By anyone's reckoning, that is very hot and very deep.

This story went down very well with the tourists. I didn't believe it for a minute but I did take the point about keeping to the path.

More uplifting was the narrow wooden bridge across the Puarenga River, where half-naked Maori children dive into the water to collect the coins thrown in by visitors. They were so lithe and beautiful, those children, with their warm coffee-coloured skin and dark intelligent eyes. Maori adults, as a rule, run to fat, as do most of the Islander people. This is probably due to an acquired Western diet of too many hamburgers and milkshakes. At any rate I never saw a thin Maori.

The journey back to Auckland was long and tiring. On arrival we had a whip-round for the driver, who had been an excellent and knowledgeable guide, then finished the day with a meal in the Town House restaurant in Queen Street. We all agreed it would be nice to meet up again some time, said goodbye, and I never saw any of them again.

There is a view shared by many overseas visitors that 'New Zealand is always closed'. In part this is due to the fact that businesses and shops are shut from Friday night until Monday morning, but also because of the frequent public holidays that New Zealanders enjoy over Christmas and the New Year. Additionally, during the summer months there are two more special holidays, Auckland Centenary Day on the 28th January, and Waitangi Day on the 6th February. Waitangi Day commemorates the signing of the treaty, in 1840, between the *pakeha* or white man, and the Maoris.

On Centenary Day I hired a car from the garage where Mariana worked and explored some unfamiliar territory north of Auckland, along the bays of the picturesque Hibiscus Coast. The prettiest place was the tiny settlement of Waiwere, yet another hot mineral spa, and it was here that I stopped for lunch.

Continuing my drive north, I ventured as far as the Satellite Tracking Station at Warkworth. This is a new telecommunications centre open to the public. I paid my entrance money and joined the small guided tour around the site, admired the hundred foot diameter dish and gazed in awe at an insignificant bleep on a screen, which I was emphatically assured was Skylab.

Then February was upon us, the hottest and most humid month and, as arranged at the New Year, Elaine Farrow came up from Taupo to stay with me. Kathleen, meanwhile, had departed on a mini-bus tour of the South Island and I was heartily glad to see her go. She and I couldn't agree on any single damn thing. If I wanted a window open, she wanted it shut. If the day was overcast, I might comment that it was going to clear up; Kathleen would insist that it was about to rain. The dissension went on and on until I was as much looking forward to her holiday as she was.

With more reason I was also in the doghouse with Anne McCowan. I had been guilty of the unforgivable crime of flooding the laundry room and its adjacent environs, namely Anne's posh kitchen. It had happened one Saturday morning while I was using the washing machine. Stupidly I forgot to connect up all the necessary plumbing to prevent such a disaster, and this was drawn to my attention – and that of the entire road I dare say – by the shrill cries that bordered on hysterics emanating from upstairs. I tore up the outside steps to find the poor woman up to her ankles in a swirling sea of soapsuds, while the wash tub thumped and shuddered, spewing out its watery innards. As if that wasn't bad enough, I spilt a huge packet of Persil into the deepening lake around us, which by that time was doing a passable impression of Niagara Falls down the stairs.

I thought Anne was going to faint.

It took nearly two hours to staunch the flow and my well-meant remarks that at least the floor would be nice and clean were not appreciated. But eventually Anne began to look a more healthy colour and I made us both a cup of tea. She sipped hers gratefully but still eyed me with a look of hurt distrust. In my more paranoid moments I actually entertained the suspicion that Kathleen had engineered the whole thing, but then decided she probably wasn't bright enough to be that devious.

When I met Elaine at the bus station, I found her bubbling over with the joys of life. I did wonder if it was a front put on for my benefit but when she happily related how she had found a nice cushy little job as a secretary with a small company in Taupo, it truly seemed that her earlier homesickness had passed. We devoted most of the day to the shops and Elaine splashed out on an outfit for herself and some things for the children. In the evening we decided to go and see a film. Elaine opted for *The Exorcist*, which was drawing big crowds in Queen Street.

'I want to see the bit where her head turns round,' she said, and so we went. The film was brilliant but even so I kept my eyes firmly shut at the nasty bits and I suspect Elaine did the same.

She had planned to stay only until the weekend but it didn't take much persuasion on my part for her to extend her visit by a couple more days until Waitangi Day. In order to make the most of a day off, I picked up a car from Mariana the previous evening and after an early breakfast, and with Elaine sharing the driving, we set off for Taupo. We made it in time for lunch and I left for Auckland again in the afternoon. The drive had exhilarated me. Even a round trip of nearly four hundred miles can be a pleasant day out on New Zealand's open and un-crowded roads.

The 1974 Commonwealth Games in Christchurch began at the end of January and monopolised our television sets for over a week. Eunice phoned to say she had spotted her cousin Jack doing his spot of adjudicating at one of the swimming events. I hadn't bothered to watch any of the Games coverage because I disliked sport, but I was looking forward to seeing the Royal Family when they sailed into Auckland aboard the *Britannia*. The good ship *Ellinis* was due in port on the same day, having completed another round trip to Southampton and back. Kerry and I intended to pay a housecall. It meant making an early start because the ship was due to dock at seven in the morning. I caught an almost empty bus and met Kerry outside the hotel. We hurried through the quiet streets but were late. This was fortunate as the *Ellinis* was late too.

As we tripped along Queen Street, one large, blue-and-white and very familiar shape hove into sight to lie alongside Princes Wharf, next to her more illustrious berth-mate, the Royal Yacht *Britannia*. We had no trouble whatsoever in getting aboard without embarkation passes. The Staff Captain, who was usually a bit of an old misery, actually smiled at us. Kerry, the two-timer, disappeared in search of Mike the steward and I didn't see her for hours.

From the Boat Deck there was a first class view of *Britannia* only a stone's throw away. It was still very early but eager crowds had gathered and were standing six deep along Quay Street waiting to see the Queen and Prince Philip leave for their walkabout in Auckland Domain. The Domain was a large area of parkland in the city centre.

The passengers and crew members standing with me on the *Ellinis* had the best view of the Royal party, however. *Ellinis*, God bless her, saluted with three deep blasts on her siren and disgorged a cloud of brown soot. I hung around the ship until late morning taking photographs of everything and everyone: Kerry by herself, Kerry with Mike, the *Britannia* (lots of pictures of *Britannia*), her Royal New Zealand Naval escorts, the *Canterbury* and the *Waikato*, and even a snap of the little Waiheke ferry for good measure.

It was really strange being back aboard the *Ellinis* again and I tried unsuccessfully not to think too much about Jan-Yves.

Marie had invited me to have lunch with her and because it was such a lovely day, I legged it all the way to Remuera. By February I was definitely starting to toughen up – yessir!

Marie's kitchen was one of my favourite places. It was more like a living room actually, large and delightfully un-modern and comfortably untidy. One wall had some built in shelves that overflowed with books, photographs and some artistic efforts by Mariana's young pupils. The big sturdy table in the middle of the room invited all to sit around it and while away an hour or so over a cup of coffee. There was also a picture of Our Lady on the wall because the Franklins were Roman Catholics. At first I thought it rather strange, but then I grew to like the picture. Though unaware of it at that time, the first seeds of my conversion to Catholicism many years later were planted in Marie Franklin's kitchen.

Les was officially retired but he still did some part-time work and when he came in for his mid-day break, Marie and I were cutting up sandwiches for lunch.

'What the dickens are you two up to? Having a picnic in the

kitchen?' he inquired gruffly. Then he went on to relate quite casually how he had crossed the path of the Royal cavalcade more than once on his morning's errands. Being Les, he was unimpressed by the bout of Royal fever that had gripped the city. Marie's face was a study in exasperation, for directly after breakfast she had deserted hearth and home to mingle with the crowds at the Domain. Being Marie, she had managed to get a good view.

There was to be a civic reception for the Queen at the Hotel Intercontinental that evening, and Kerry was to be on duty. For this occasion she had spent the whole afternoon at the hairdressers. She had slimmed down considerably since returning home, and now she looked very glamorous and grown-up for such an important function.

Another large crowd had gathered in the evening sunshine to see the Royal Family depart the *Britannia*. I nudged my way into a good vantage point on the quayside, quite close to the gangway, and shortly before eight-thirty the Queen appeared wearing an emerald gown and, of course, a tiara. The crowd reserved its most enthusiastic response for Princess Anne, the bride of a couple of months, and her husband Captain Mark Phillips, who gave a self-conscious little wave. Everyone cheered the louder.

I couldn't help but notice that this latest addition to the Royal Family had rapidly acquired his father-in-law's habit of walking with his hands clasped firmly behind his back.

In the midst of all the excitement, *Ellinis* weighed anchor and soon after was making dignified headway out into the open sea at the start of a Pacific island cruise, with Los Angeles as her final destination.

Only three weeks later I was again back at the quayside to witness yet another departure. I was beginning thoroughly to detest the sight of passenger ships, as all they ever did was take people away. First of all Jan-Yves and now, at the end of February and on the eve of my twentieth birthday, Philip Franklin, who was sailing to Singapore. From there he was scheduled to fly to Paris, and then to London. I gave him my parents' address and he promised to visit and assure them that their errant child was alive, very well and having the time of her life down and almost under, in New Zealand.

'But for heaven's sake don't mention anything about Jan-Yves,' I reminded Philip, my confidant. I went on to ply him with extravagant instructions as to how best find his way from the heart of London into Essex, which he endured with good humour and tolerance.

I felt awfully intrusive being with Philip's family at that – for them – sad time, but Marie had asked me to come. Both she and Les put on brave faces but I could barely imagine what they really felt, watching their elder son sailing away for goodness knows how long in order to pursue his chosen career. Until then, it had never occurred to me how similarly my own family must have felt about my departure.

There was a half-open gate across the wharf beyond the official buildings. With one mind, Philip's mother and I ignored the notice proclaiming 'No Unauthorised Entry' and walked together the full length of the quay until we could go no further without getting our feet wet. We could see Philip clearly where he stood on the deck, waving at us as the ship inched its way towards open water.

Only when it was impossible to make out any figures clearly, did we turn back. I took hold of Marie's arm and we walked slowly towards the others and the waiting car.

CHAPTER XII

Wellington

LESS THAN A WEEK after Philip's departure for Europe, Richard, who had passed his school finals, left for Dunedin, where he had been accepted at the medical school. Now that her family was depleted by two-thirds, Marie channelled her copious energies into two demanding activities. The first was to devote a couple of hours each day to teaching English to the Islander children at the local Roman Catholic infant school. The other work was to arrange a lecture tour for a professor of music whom she had met in England. This professor specialised in music therapy for deaf and autistic children and was coming to New Zealand to advance this work. For Marie, it turned out to be a very time-consuming commitment, so on some evenings I went to help out with the typing.

Marie Franklin's kind heart sometimes got the better of her. For example, she and Mariana had been talked into making regular visits to a querulous old lady who lived out in the sticks and kept ducks for company – in the kitchen. The old lady scorned the use of banks or post office and insisted on keeping all her savings stuffed in an old paper bag and hidden in the Aga. She would pass around tea in dirty cups and generous slices of musty cherry cake, which, not liking to refuse, Mariana once crammed down the sides of her wellington boots until she got outside.

I never did hear what Marie had done with her cherry cake.

As a break from all these good works, one Sunday afternoon the four of us, Marie and Les, Mariana and myself, went for a long drive through the Waitakere Hills to look at the surfing beaches on the west coast. The twisting dirt road passed through some fine examples of native bush. The 'bush' in New Zealand consists, not of arid grasslands, as in Australia or South Africa, but of a lush abundance of green vegetation: towering kauri trees, totari and tree ferns, here and there splashed with the warm vibrant colours of flowering shrubs. On that particular day there had been a welcome downpour of heavy rain and the trees steamed in the sunshine, the foliage smelling refreshingly damp.

Piha Beach, some thirty miles west of Auckland, is an isolated but popular surfing beach where rough seas are guaranteed and the great white breakers crash on to the sands. The sand is black because of its high content of iron-ore but it is very pleasant to walk on, unlike the sharp rocks that Mariana led me on to. We clambered out to meet the waves that rose and fell in the narrow gullies and soaked our legs and skirts.

On the journey home the car started making very anti-social noises, stalled a couple of times, and then drifted to a halt. Les got out and peered under the bonnet for some minutes. He diagnosed ignition failure. This apparently was one of Philip's less successful mechanical adjustments. Les fiddled at length but without much conviction while his wife remarked quietly to me, 'He doesn't have a clue as to what he's doing, you know.'

It seemed a sensible course of action for the females of the party to keep quiet and feign indifference. We admired the view until the engine spluttered into life under protest. Les slammed down the bonnet, we all jumped back in and proceeded home with caution.

One weekend in the middle of March, while the weather was still pleasantly warm, the bank where I worked in Avondale held its grand annual barbecue. The venue for this event was the country home of one of the staff, a lady called Margaret Langdon. Margaret loved organising things; she was a stalwart of the local Womens' Institute and a veteran of cricket teas.

It was more of a pool party than a mere barbecue, though there was plenty of good food and drink. Margaret's swimming pool was big enough actually to swim in and was surrounded by an attractive patio and a fenced wind-break. Her house, like so many of the more expensive properties in Auckland, was built up high over the garage and a huge room known as the 'rumpus room'. This was used as a playroom, workshop and, more importantly, a bar.

All the rooms upstairs opened out on to a balcony.

As the party progressed, anyone who had not yet been into the pool of their own volition was given a helping hand or two, fully dressed or not. Margaret was hard put to find enough dry clothes to put the girls in. When everyone had more or less dried out, we all trooped upstairs to watch the new colour television.

Watching television in New Zealand must surely be the last resort of the unimaginative or the physically housebound. There was only one channel, and it transmitted a mixture of American and British programmes. Most were hopelessly out of date and on a bad night the discerning viewer could be faced with a year-old episode of *Coronation Street*, an even older edition of *Z Cars*, or a tantalising re-run of *The Lucy Show.* I remained unconvinced that the addition of colour would turn any of the above into compulsive viewing. It was no wonder that the local cinemas did so well.

The following Monday morning there was an impromptu jumble sale in the bank, when Margaret emptied out two large carrier bags containing various bits of peoples' property, including some mismatched sandals and socks, my cigarette lighter and a bra that no-one was brave enough to claim.

B.J. summoned me for dictation. I had quickly trained him to my school of thought regarding the duties of a secretary, and after my first week, had flatly refused to have anything more to do with the dictaphone. I wondered idly if he had much recollection of the previous evening, when he had spent the better part of an hour slumped on a stool at Margaret's bar telling me how *very* much he had always liked English girls. He emphasised his point by placing one hand on my leg.

'Oh, do behave yourself, B.J.', I had said as I removed his hand as discreetly as I could. Men are such fools.

Now he grinned at me sheepishly across the debris on his desk and stirred three spoonfuls of sugar into his black coffee. I sipped at my third cup of the morning.

My mother had very definite ideas about most things, and one of them was black coffee. She had never approved of me drinking the stuff and maintained that it smacked too much of hangovers and fast living. I suspect that in her mind the habit went hand in hand with another undesirable trait of modern young girls, namely not wearing a vest. Anyway, B.J. and I enjoyed our black coffee together.

He indicated the growing pile of files on the desk, that promised to avalanche on to the floor at any minute.

'Oh God, what a day!' he declared languidly. 'There's all this lot and then those people are coming in from Titirangi and then . . .'

'Don't worry about it, B.J.', I soothed, 'She'll be right!'

Two well-known celebrities visited Auckland towards the end of March and I saw them both. One was a lady called Eleanor Hibbert, but known to her millions of readers as Jean Plaidy, the historical romance writer. She visited a book shop in the city to sign copies of her latest book, a novel about Prince Albert.

The other was David Cassidy, teeny-bopper, heart-throb and superstar, who arrived at the airport with a face lopsided and swollen from the effects of a cholera vaccination. He was greeted by hundreds of screaming fans. I screamed at him too at one of his open air concerts in Eden Park. I had to go alone as I couldn't talk anyone else into accompanying me.

By way of contrast, Mariana Franklin obtained tickets for the Royal New Zealand Ballet, appearing in Auckland to perform Stravinsky's *Firebird* and a noisy, crashing piece by Benjamin Britten. We went to the Saturday matinee and enjoyed ourselves immensely.

In spite of its relatively small population of about half a million, the city of Auckland could provide a wide variety of entertainment and night life. Apart from the one disco I mentioned before, there were live shows, first-class restaurants, and a plethora of cinemas ranging from the plush multi-screen complexes in Queen Street to the small suburban fleapits, where the seating was sometimes little better than miserably upholstered benches. At any rate, admission prices were always reasonable and on average I went to see two films each week.

Another attractive feature was the futuristic shopping 'cities', with fashion stores and supermarkets all under one roof. They were built out in the suburbs as an alternative to the busy city centre. There was one near Mount Albert called St Luke's, a fantasia of glass and escalators, fountains, sculptures, shopping malls and galleries.

On the debit side was the Auckland Regional Authority transport system. Frankly the bus service was diabolical. All routes led into the city centre and then out of it, but there were no means of travelling by bus directly across the city. They were nearly all trolley buses and, like their London Transport cousins, were of a gregarious nature and preferred to travel in convoys of three or more. On a sharp bend or a bumpy piece of road it was usual for the trolley poles to fall off the overhead cables and the driver was obliged to run round to the rear of his vehicle to reconnect them.

There was also an inter-suburban railway, so cleverly hidden away from public view that it was almost a year before I discovered it.

Cars are very expensive in New Zealand, so much so that it was sometimes cheaper to buy a car in the United Kingdom and pay to have it shipped out. The ratio of car drivers per head of population was high and, as the legal age for holding a licence was only fifteen, it was not unusual to see youngsters driving themselves to school wearing uniform and ankle socks.

Easter was late that year, not until the middle of April, so I decided to take advantage of the long weekend break and visit Wellington. I'd kept in touch with a crowd of girls from the *Ellinis* who had come out to New Zealand on a subsidised scheme to work for the government in the capital. As they were living in hostels, it wasn't possible for me to stay with them, so I made a reservation at a hotel and caught the long distance bus from Auckland very early on Easter Saturday. It was nearly five hundred miles to Wellington and a journey of about twelve hours.

The road to Taupo I knew quite well by now, of course, but from there on it was all new ground. Mount Ngauruhoe, an active volcano a few miles south of Lake Taupo, had been erupting on and off for the past two months and was still smoking gustily as the bus crossed through the Tongariro National Park. Because of the unusually dry summer, the land was parched brown and the shortage of good grass had forced many dairy farmers to 'dry out' their herds. Another effect of the long drought was the low water level in Lake Taupo. This had dropped almost to a critical level and as the water in this lake was the source of power for the Turangi hydro-electric scheme, power cuts had resulted.

I saw fit not to mention any of this in my letters home. Power cuts were the prerogative of strike-torn Britain on its three-day working week, not golden, sun-baked New Zealand.

Total darkness had fallen long before the bus reached Wellington, so all I could make out of the capital city was a confusion of high buildings and lights. As it was late, I took a taxi from the bus station to the Hotel St George, where I had made my reservation. This turned out to be one of the most exclusive establishments in town with a very expensive restaurant, but I discovered a health food restaurant just along the street and there I had a meal of mixed salad with beansprouts and a couple of thick slices of dark, home-baked rye bread.

After the long journey I was much too tired to go anywhere else, so I returned to the hotel. My room was enormous but cold. The heating wouldn't come on so in desperation I switched on my hair dryer to generate some warmth. Then I got into bed and wrote letters on the hotel's posh, headed paper.

The next day was wet and miserable. Because it was Sunday, there wasn't much to do except explore the city on foot and gaze in closed shop windows. There was one coffee shop open doing a roaring trade serving tourists and locals alike, trying to find somewhere out of the cold.

There is a well known saying in New Zealand that you can always identify a Wellingtonian by the way he walks, with head and shoulders thrust forward and a hand held on to his hat because of the wind. That day Wellington lived up to its blustery reputation, with a bitter cold wind blowing in from the south, bringing squally showers with it. I was spoilt, having known nothing but warm, dry weather ever since arriving in Auckland back in November, and the capital's autumn climate came as something of a shock.

Back at the hotel, the friends I had arranged to meet up with were waiting for me. They had brought their own food with them so we went upstairs to my room. I ordered hot drinks from room service and the remainder of the day passed more pleasantly as we swapped travellers' tales sitting on the floor and spread delicious pâté on to chunks of crusty bread.

None of them liked Wellington at all as it rained most of the time and was rather strait-laced, not like cosmopolitan Auckland. Apartments were expensive to rent and even harder to come by, and the hostels supplied by the New Zealand government were stark and hopelessly inadequate.

'It's worse than being back at school,' a girl from Edinburgh moaned.

On Easter Monday the rain reluctantly eased off a little and when the clouds broke, it was possible to make out the steep hills behind the city. Most of the flat land in and around Wellington had been reclaimed from the sea to provide a level base for the many high-rise office blocks crowded near the harbour. What with the hills and the buildings, I found it very claustrophobic, but, encouraged by the watery sun, I took some photographs of the Government buildings and Parliament House, uninspiring Victorian piles of dark grey stone.

The Kelburn cable car was nice, though, rising in just a few minutes up a steep gradient to five hundred feet above sea level. The view from the summit was impressive even on such a dreary day and showed the city to its best advantage, the harbour too, and beyond it, Cook Strait and a misty hump that was the South Island.

In the afternoon the heavens opened again and convinced me that I had had quite enough of Wellington. I booked a ticket for the overnight sleeper train to Auckland, the *Silver Star*, that departed daily at eight o'clock. This was fabulous, a silver, streamlined Japanese train similar to the 'bullet' design ones. I had a compact single compartment with a bed that pulled down from the wall, a micro-sized shower unit and a loo.

As soon as the train was clear of Wellington and its suburbs, I took myself off to the restaurant car for dinner. The meal was excellent and as I was on my own, I propped a book open on the table and read through four courses.

Next morning I awoke to bright sunshine. The train was only a few miles short of Auckland and I felt as though I had been away for ages. The *Silver Star* drew into the long platform alongside its stable-mate, the *Silver Fern*, that provided the inter-city daytime service. In view of the fact that it was still very early, I decided to go first to the Hotel Intercontinental for breakfast. Not to the restaurant though – I bought some fruit and yoghurt and sneaked up the staff stairs to Kerry's room. I wasn't supposed to be there, of course, but that had never stopped me.

I tapped on the door. 'Hi, it's me. Are you alone?'

The door was flung open. 'Bloody cheek! Of course I'm alone. Where the hell have you been *this* time?' Kerry was half dressed and struggling into her tights.

'Wellington. It was horrible.' I sat down and carefully peeled the top off the yoghurt. 'Gotta spoon?'

She threw me a nasty tea-stained piece of cutlery and continued dressing. 'I haven't got time to talk to you, I'm on duty in ten minutes,' she said. 'Incidentally do you *ever* go to work?'

'Not until tomorrow. I thought I might go down to the beach this morning. Will it be all right to leave my things here?'

'If you must. Listen, I've got a break at twelve for a couple of hours. Come back here for lunch. My mother's coming.'

This was a bolt from the blue for I couldn't remember Kerry ever mentioning having a mother before. I'd always assumed she'd been hatched from an egg.

'Mum and Dad have been separated for ages', she explained offhandedly. 'Now she wants a divorce and she's coming to live in Auckland. Oh Lord, I hope she doesn't expect me to go and live with her,' she added in sudden horror.

Then she checked her watch, swore at the time, and prepared to rush off madly, as the saying goes, in all directions. 'Don't you forget, Wendy. You be here at twelve!'

I walked to Mission Bay, which was miles away, so by the time I got there it was almost time to turn back. I dutifully returned to the hotel at lunch-time as directed, to meet Kerry. She introduced me to her mother, a smart, blonde older edition of Kerry herself, but much harder. She gushed and charmed all through the meal that she insisted on paying for, and talked at length about her future plans. Kerry was unusually subdued and it occurred to me that she need have no fear that this self-assured and very attractive woman, who could hardly be more than forty, had any intention of setting up house with a grown-up daughter.

I frequently reflected on the complexity of mother-and-daughter relationships. There were Kerry and her mother, superficially so alike yet warily measuring each other up like rivals; Marie and Mariana, also very alike and with such an acute rapport that it often appeared one knew what the other was thinking; and then myself and my own mother, who never knew what I was thinking, which, all things considered, was probably just as well.

If I ever have children, I think I shall go for the boys, I decided.

I said goodbye to Kerry and her mother and went home. The bus dropped me at the stop in Mount Albert Road, just across the road from the house, and I walked unhurriedly towards the drive. I paused for a moment at the gate and fumbled deep in my bag for my keys. At that time of day I knew the house would be empty and just as surely I suddenly knew that I was not alone. When I looked up I saw a man lying on the grass with his arms folded behind his head. He sat up as I approached.

My insides did a somersault. It was Jan-Yves.

CHAPTER XIII

The Return of Jan-Yves

I WASN'T AT ALL CERTAIN whether or not I was pleased to see him. I can remember asking myself angrily, 'Why does this man always show up when I'm in such a mess?' Two days in wet and windy Wellington had wrought havoc with my hair, which was of the type that looked fantastic when the rollers were taken out, then reverted to its natural rat tails as soon as a breeze got up. I felt scruffy, extremely cranky, and with the threat of a headache, which didn't help.

However, I couldn't have looked quite as bad as all that, for I was soon smothered in a huge hug and kissed for at least five minutes, just as in the films.

A little voice at the back of my mind wondered about the neighbours – then I forgot all about the neighbours . . .

When we had finished for the moment, we both started talking at once.

'Jan-Yves, what are you doing here?'

'Where *have* you been all day?'

'How long have you been waiting?'

'Since last night,' Jan-Yves started to explain when I finally let him. 'I flew into Auckland just before midnight and I phoned you from the airport. I even tried phoning you from Los Angeles but you weren't here. You're never here, girl!'

'What on earth were you doing in Los Angeles?'

'Will you let me finish? I decided to fly home at the last minute so there wasn't time to write to you. There was a stopover in L.A. so I called you and spoke to the lady upstairs and she said you'd gone away. Anyway, I came over this morning and you still weren't here so I went away and came back about an hour ago. Now, where have you been?'

'Wellington, actually.'

'Wellington! That's a bloody awful place.'

'Yes, Jan-Yves, I'm only too well aware of Wellington's shortcomings. Oh, let's go in. I'm simply gasping for a cup of tea. I had lunch with Kerry and she never stops talking. Do you remember Kerry?

'Your blonde friend with the big tits – how could I forget her?'

'Exactly. Anyway, I've had a double dose because her mother was there as well. Oh, Jan-Yves, I know you said you might come to see me, but I didn't really think you would.' I linked my arm through his and pulled him towards the house.

He appeared amused by my scepticism. 'Funny girl!'

While he made himself at home on the settee, I emptied cold, soggy teabags out of the pot (Kathleen never emptied a teapot) and took some time to study Jan-Yves closely. He seemed larger than I remembered, observed in the close confines of the flat. His hair was longer and he had grown a beard. In fact he looked like a Viking.

Over the tea, Jan-Yves explained that he could stay for about a week before he was due back in Sydney for the start of the next term. He had missed out on a whole three months' study time and was eager to go back. He was staying in a house shared by an old student friend in Ponsonby, which was one of the older parts of Auckland, popular with the Polynesian people, students and drop-outs.

I didn't hesitate when Jan-Yves asked me to stay with him, but re-packed a suitcase and left a note for Kathleen in case she missed me, together with my contribution to the week's rent. I moved in with my boyfriend to a dilapidated bungalow in Ponsonby for one short week of living in sin.

This was the nearest I ever got to living in a commune. The bungalow was large and rambling, and built of weather-board that creaked when the wind blew. A shaky veranda ran all round the house and creaked whether the wind blew or not. There was a constant coming and going of occupants, the only permanent resident being a middle-aged hippie called Karmel, who wore faded and fraying shorts and a Maori good luck charm called a *tiki* around his neck.

Jan-Yves' friend had gone away for a few days and so we had his room, sparingly furnished with a double bed and with some home-grown art on the walls. It smelled strongly of joss-sticks.

My biggest worry was that I might be expected to smoke 'pot', but as it turned out, no-one ever asked me. I felt over-dressed and over-employed because I was the only one to have a proper job. In spite of these handicaps, everyone was very friendly and kind in an abstract sort of way, and thankfully left Jan-Yves and me alone. We made love every night, then in the cold reality of day I would leave Jan-Yves still in bed and dash bleary-eyed off to work. From Ponsonby that meant two extra bus changes, so I was usually late. Every lunch hour I spent on the phone chatting to Jan-Yves, to the obvious approval of the rest of the bank staff. Every evening I hurried back to Ponsonby in time to go out for a meal or see a film.

We argued quite a bit; I insisted on paying for my share of everything while Jan-Yves insisted on paying for both of us. I said angrily that this arrangement was old-fashioned and unnecessary considering *I* was the one working. At the weekend I turned the tables on him by turning up with a rental car and whisking him off on a quick tour of Thames and the Coromandel Peninsula. Jan-Yves was not keen on driving and also detested flying. By the time we got home, he had a phobia about cars too.

'I don't know what's worse,' he muttered ashen-faced, 'sitting in an aeroplane or going out motoring with you.'

I gave him a sharp pinch in what passed for affection. 'Now that's a funny thing. It's the first time I've ever been likened to a jumbo jet.'

We had one major disagreement just before Jan-Yves left for Sydney. He wanted me to go with him and I was determined to stay put. God knows, I wanted to be with him, but I dug my heels in because I wasn't ready to throw away everything I had achieved over the last few months, my precious independence, my job and my friends. Not just yet.

Jan-Yves argued and pleaded, and finally slammed the door and disappeared for several hours. When he returned, he sat talking on the veranda to Karmel for ages and pointedly ignored me when I joined them. Not wanting to spoil our last day together, I weakened and compromised.

'I'll come over in a few months – promise.'

'I've no doubt that you'll do whatever you want to do,' Jan-Yves replied shortly but he looked happier, and I felt better too.

He had a mid-morning flight the following day but being an emotional coward, I refused to go to the airport to see him off. I went into work as usual, kept one eye on the clock and snapped everyone's head off who dared to speak to me. The time of his departure came and went. I called the airport to check that the flight had taken off on time. It had.

I day-dreamed through the remainder of the day with a weight like a solid chunk of lead at the back of my throat, dreading the moment when I should have to go back alone to the flat in Mount Albert and endure Kathleen's irritating and banal conversation. However, what I did find when I got home was Frank and Eunice's old car parked outside, with May and Jack, fresh up from the South Island, sitting in the back. They all looked so comfortingly familiar that I returned their hugs with interest.

May looked rather peaky and she carried her arm in a sling, for she had cracked a bone while pushing a relative's toddler on a swing. She had been forced to stay in and around Christchurch for several weeks to receive the necessary hospital treatment. But in spite of her accident, she and Jack had thoroughly enjoyed their trip and now planned to base themselves in Auckland and see something of the north. It was only a couple more weeks before they were due to sail home on the *Ellinis*.

Eunice tried to persuade me to go back to One Tree Hill with them for a meal but I couldn't face that. I wanted to be left alone to think about Jan-Yves and be miserable. When the four of them had gone, I thanked my stars that my normally home-loving flat-mate was having an evening out for once so that I could pathetically wallow in a mental re-run of the past week and a tortuous analysis of what *he* could really have meant when he said such-and-such a thing, and whether I had made the right decision about not going with him. Probably not.

I wondered if Jan-Yves would phone me when he reached Sydney, but though I stared long and reproachfully at the telephone, it didn't ring.

The following weekend I was still missing Jan-Yves. The thought of being cooped up indoors was unbearable so I booked a car out again, taking care to fill up with petrol on the Friday night as, due to government restrictions, no petrol stations were permitted to open at the weekend. This practice was not a regular New Zealand quirk, just a result of the international fuel crisis. This was 1974 and things were bad. As a method of rationing fuel it was utterly useless, because everyone bought all the petrol they needed on weekdays.

I neither knew nor cared where I was going so I headed south on State Highway One as far as Hamilton. This was New Zealand's biggest inland city, built on the great Waikato River. From Hamilton I turned due east and wandered across country, taking several wrong turnings. In truth I suppose they were not really wrong turnings, as I didn't have a specific destination in mind, but twice I ended up on dirt roads heading towards great flocks of sheep, so it seemed judicious to turn around. I must have seen several million sheep that day but no people, and that suited me just fine.

Nightfall came early, by which time I was well and truly lost. The car started to splutter, then lost power altogether, and cruised to a standstill along the grass verge. It didn't take long, even for a mechanical greenhorn such as myself, to figure out the cause of the trouble. Little Miss Know-all had run out of bloody petrol. Seeing that I had covered the best part of two hundred miles on my haphazard wanderings, and that it was only a little car, to run out of gas was hardly surprising.

I consulted the map by the pale glow of my lighter and calculated that the nearest town was some twenty miles away and bore the unlikely name of Matamata.

Christ, what a country!

When my eyes became night-acclimatised, I thought I could make out a faint light not too far away. There was nothing else for it but to get out and investigate.

It was a horrible walk. I could barely see where I was going and, it being the end of April, it was starting to get very cold at night. My thin jacket was totally inadequate. But nearly a mile along the road I came to a small batch of houses and a general store, closed for the night of course. There was a single old-fashioned petrol pump on the forecourt, but though I knocked on the door for several minutes, there was no reply.

Then I tried the house next door, which in this case was about twenty yards further along the road. A young woman came to the door with a toddler supported on her hip and another child clutching at her jeans. I explained my predicament and asked if I could possibly buy a can of petrol.

She immediately invited me to come in, saying that she wasn't certain about the petrol but when her husband came home she was sure something could be sorted out. Her name was Irene, she said, and she showed me into a cosy kitchen-cum-living room. Two young collies flew out of their basket under the table to greet me like a long-lost friend. Irene plonked the toddler back into his highchair, where he set to, making short, messy work of his supper of fish fingers and chips. I sat down in a well-worn armchair beside an open log fire and gratefully sipped the coffee Irene made me. Presently she excused herself, saying she had to put the children to bed, and told me to make myself comfortable. One of the puppies scratched at my legs so I lifted her on to my lap and cuddled her.

Some time later Irene came back and then her husband, whose name was Colin, returned. We explained my problem and they discussed how best I could be helped. Colin said that he didn't have enough spare fuel to siphon any off for me, at least not enough to get very far. The man who ran the general store was away for the evening, but he could be relied upon to bend the rules and serve me some petrol in the morning – which meant, of course, that I should have to stay there for the night. I felt a complete idiot, which I was, and they agreed with me. We all laughed and Irene insisted that I wouldn't be any trouble; they had a spare room and there was no more to be said about it.

I learned that Irene and Colin were still considered as newcomers to the community, having moved out from Auckland a year or so before to start their own small holding and for Irene to establish her own interest of breeding show collies. That evening they had been invited to a party at a farm somewhere out in the hills, and they assured me it would be perfectly all right if I went along with them.

I've no idea where that party was. We travelled for miles along a blind, twisting lane that climbed steeply until we came to an isolated farmhouse with about a dozen vehicles, mostly station wagons, already parked in the yard. Inside, the house was bursting at the seams; there were people packed into the hall and all over the stairs, and of course, crowding into the kitchen. I was soon separated from my new friends but everyone else was very friendly. I found a full glass of something pushed into one hand and a plate of cold chicken and salad into the other. They were all local farming people and most of the talk was of sheep, the continuing drought, sheep, the Government, the E.E.C., sheep, horses (here I was on more familiar ground) and still more sheep. At one point Irene caught my eye across the road and mouthed 'All right?' I nodded back furiously.

Farming folk keep early hours, so we left just after midnight. I was very, very tipsy and the clear, cold air nearly knocked me for six. Irene wasn't in much better shape and we sat together giggling in the back of the car while Colin drove cautiously home.

When I went up to the spare room, I found that Irene had thoughtfully placed a hot-water bottle in the bed and laid out a night-dress. I climbed gratefully under the covers and fell asleep almost immediately. First thing next morning, Colin took me to rescue my abandoned car. He attached a tow-rope and I followed slowly behind his truck to the general store, where the proprietor was already serving a couple of other customers with illicit petrol. So much for Government regulations!

Before I left, Colin explained exactly where I was, which according to the map was almost exactly in the middle of nowhere. I thanked them both warmly for their kindness and hospitality and they stood at the fence to wave me off, the two dogs jumping at their heels.

It was a long drive home and by the time I had deposited the car at the rental agency and caught the bus to Mount Albert, it was almost dark. Kathleen was curled up in her favourite armchair and doing justice to a large box of chocolates. In between mouthfuls, she told me exactly what she thought of me – my scandalous behaviour with Jan-Yves (I told her to mind her own business), and my recklessness in gallivanting around the country and staying out all night (here I conceded she had a point). Having got all that off her chest, she flounced into the kitchen, switched on the oven and began viciously pricking sausages for her dinner.

A couple of weeks later I was delighted to receive a letter from Philip Franklin, who was now firmly established in Kuwait and settling in to his work. He reported that he had been to visit my parents while he was in England – in spite of my directions. This I already knew, as my mother had written glowingly about 'that nice boy, Philip'. The other 'nice boy', Richard, was also sending letters home to his family, characteristically long, scrawling bulletins, totally different from his elder brother's neatly written and precise narratives.

On the day prior to the departure of my old sailing companions, May, Jack and company on the *Ellinis*, I had a phone call from Eunice, in itself quite a normal occurrence, for Eunice was a great one for gossiping at length on the phone. On this occasion, however, what followed was an extraordinary conversation with cousin Sarah, also in temporary residence at One Tree Hill. I hadn't seen Sarah since last November and was surprised that she had asked to talk to me. She was a dry old stick by all accounts, but she could be very kind once you broke through her rather forbidding, school-marm exterior. However she was very hard of hearing, particularly over the telephone. I asked her lots of questions about her trip around the South Island, and the Commonwealth Games and received a great deal of information back. A geography lesson, in fact, leaving me in no doubt that she had *done* the South Island with monstrous thoroughness. Not once, though, did she actually answer any of my questions, or at least, not in the order I had asked them. Still, I think I was able successfully to convey the message that I would be there to see them off the next evening.

The following day and aboard *Ellinis* yet again, this time saddled with two of May's carrier bags full of last-minute shopping and souvenirs. Down below I encountered Mike the steward, still eagerly looking for Kerry. He looked so disappointed when I explained that she wasn't with me this time. Kerry really could be a bitch.

'She does have a boyfriend, Mike,' I said. 'Forget about her.'

He shook his head. 'No, she come home to Greece. We marry and she like it there.'

I shrugged. After all, I had tried.

May and Sarah were back in our old cabin, which looked more gloomy than ever.

'Do you wish you were coming with us?' May teased.

'No way!' I said and meant it.

The announcements over the loudspeakers were coming thick and fast. *All ashore who's going ashore.* Naturally none of the on-board visitors took the slightest notice. After all, it was much more fun to rush off the gangways at the very last minute. When the ship eventually sailed, only one hour late this time, I went back with Eunice and Frank for a late supper. Then, bracing myself against what seemed to be an inevitable collision, I permitted the tearaway Frank to drive me home.

CHAPTER XIV

Doctors, Dentists, and Other Good Works

IT WAS NOW NEARLY a month since Jan-Yves had returned to Australia and, following an initial silence of several days, he had phoned me. He said he was very busy with his college work and had taken on a part-time tutoring job as well. Still, he usually wrote about once a week.

One month after our romantic sojourn at the house in Ponsonby, and, after counting and recounting days (I am numerically dyslexic) and making constant references to the calendar, I had every reason to believe I was pregnant. I was almost tearing my hair out by the roots with the worry, although I kept telling myself over and over again that it couldn't have happened. We had taken some basic precautions and apart from missing a second period, I felt fine. Taking solitary refuge in Avondale's small public library during my lunch hour, I delved deep into all the available books on the subject but what I learned there did nothing to reassure me. Sex results in babies.

I considered buying a do-it-yourself testing kit at the chemist but when I went into the shop I got cold feet, because the man behind the counter was a customer at the bank and knew me, so I bought some aspirin instead.

I casually raised the matter one morning over coffee, then shut up when Mrs Margaret Langdon gave me a long, hard look. When Eunice phoned one day, I almost blurted out the whole story to her but thought better of it. And as for Marie – Marie was Catholic and if the worst had happened, I just didn't know how I would face Marie.

Thinking that perhaps violent exercise might help to get things going, I took to running around the block every evening, followed by vigorous jumps in the back garden. Kathleen must have thought I was quite mad. When that didn't work, I prayed earnestly: *Dear God, please may everything be all right, please, PLEASE.*

I promise I will devote the rest of my life to good works and never, ever do IT again.

In desperation, I sneaked guiltily into the doctor's surgery. He was Scottish and elderly. Bored, he pulled my lower eyelids down and commented that I was seriously anaemic. As to the other business, it was too early to tell and I should come back in a week – with a specimen.

I didn't need to. The relief was so overwhelming that I was the sweetest girl in the whole of Auckland for at least two days. I was kind to Kathleen, bought and shared a huge box of chocolates around the bank and volunteered to stay late to help B.J. Two dollars bought me a large bottle of iron tablets from the chemist, and a short phone call arranged an appointment at the family planning clinic in Auckland's Karangahape Road.

This was the mid-seventies and I had no intention of ever living through another few weeks like that again. I would do what everyone else was doing and go on the Pill.

Mid-winter in Auckland is similar to a cool summer's day in England. The days were usually mild enough to go about coatless, though I observed that many of the native population tended to wrap up more than I did. I prided myself on being a tough Brit and made the most of the pleasant June sunshine. 1974 was an exceptionally warm year though, and the skiing season down in the South Island was delayed because of the paltriness of the available snow. At night it was cold enough to need a fire, or, as I should say, a *heater*, electric or otherwise. As Les Franklin once took pains to explain to me, there is a difference. Domestic fires are always referred to as heaters. There is only one type of *fire* in New Zealand and that is the bush fire. Announce that you have a 'fire' in the living room and the fire brigade will arrive to put it out.

Only too frequently, the city fire appliances would be called out to deal with domestic fires of another kind that threatened to burn down the homes of the Islander immigrants. On many Pacific Islands where these people originated, sophisticated Western cooking and heating apparatus was unknown, so it was not surprising that some of the less well-assimilated Islanders ignored the unfamiliar electric stove in the kitchen and simply lit their cooking fires in the middle of the floor.

They were an eye-catching people, the Fijians and the Samoans, and never more so than when turned out in their Sunday best. They were devout churchgoers, Baptists mainly, and filled the Sunday buses on their way to church. The women wore flamboyant cotton frocks, as garishly coloured and patterned as possible, with absurdly large straw hats gaily decorated with cheap plastic flowers. The men favoured a combination of ethnic and Western dress, such as wrap-over calf-length skirts and bare legs, topped by a shirt and jacket. As a race, obesity was widespread among them.

To the casual observer there was no racial disharmony in New Zealand; it was very rare to hear a white New Zealander speak ill of a Maori. The Maoris and the Islanders tended to be employed in the more menial jobs, however. Even so, co-existing as they did in the *pakeha*'s world, the Maoris retained a fierce pride in their own culture.

Once I heard a distinguished Maori educationalist say that the New Zealand Government had the best propaganda machine in the world. I can only comment that I never once met a Maori socially, nor did I ever work with one.

Towards the end of June I became reluctantly involved in the inauguration of a new womens' organisation. This was the brainchild of one of the bank's regular customers, a small, dark and dynamic lady called Melva Scott, who grabbed me one day as I was about to go out for lunch. She artfully wheedled me into going along to her house for the first meeting to take the minutes. In no way was I keen on the idea, but having that morning received a particularly loving letter from Jan-Yves, I was well disposed to the world in general and in any case I was no match for Melva's persuasiveness and charm.

The handful of similarly press-ganged recruits who attended that first meeting had little or no idea as to what we were about. We gathered around the big dining room table in Melva's Glen Eden home, drinking cups of tea while our hostess enthusiastically expounded her ideas.

'What I had in mind,' she explained, 'was a social gathering for women of all ages to meet, say once a month, for a meal at a hotel somewhere, and then have a speaker on some topical issue, to be followed by a debate.' This was received with rustling murmurs of approval.

'I do believe that what we want is something a little more stimulating than the sort of things dished out at the W.I.,' she concluded. More murmurs of assent while I pulled a face and scribbled it all down.

Having obtained the unanimous consent of the gathered company to go ahead, Melva began delegating jobs. To me she handed a large sheet of paper. It was a list of names, including those of the editor of a popular women's magazine, a local politician, a representative of the pro-abortion campaign and several well-known feminist writers. They were all such terrifying and enterprising women, and I wondered maliciously why Melva Scott's name wasn't among them.

That lady smiled sweetly at me.

'Wendy dear, can you write to all of these people and make some provisional bookings?'

Wendy smiled sweetly back and said she would. *Oh lord, what am I letting myself in for?*

We were plied with more tea and home-made cakes and then sent on our way.

The first monthly meeting, a couple of weeks later, received an encouraging response, with an attendance of about fifty, ranging in age from seventeen to seventy. Some of these were women who had hardly been out anywhere by themselves socially for many years. While New Zealand may have been the first country to give women the vote, it was still a strictly male-dominated society – and over-ripe for change.

Our guest speaker was the women's magazine editor, who was a personal acquaintance of the resolute Melva. She was an immaculately groomed feminist in her early forties, who oozed self-confidence and called herself 'Ms'. After she had finished speaking on her feminist principles and provoked a lively discussion, she took me aside.

'What you must do now is write up an interesting account of my talk and submit it to the press. Can you do that?' She smiled at me encouragingly.

'Well actually, I've never . . .' I demurred.

'I know you haven't but I saw you taking notes, so you shouldn't have too much trouble. And if you do need some help, you can call me.' She handed me her card. 'Good luck.'

I sat up in bed late that night writing up my notes. I typed and re-typed them first thing next morning, submitted them to the *Auckland Star*, and had the pleasure of seeing my first published article a few days later.

From then on Melva Scott's *Western District's Women's Dinner Club* went from strength to strength and after a few months was attracting a membership of nearly two hundred. I continued doing the press releases and dabbled on the fringes of the Women's Movement.

I tried unsuccessfully to persuade Kerry to come to a meeting.

She made a face. 'You mean it's *all* women? No, I don't think so.'

I said, 'Women do have a lot to offer each other, you know,' but Kerry remained unconvinced.

'Frankly, I'd have thought *you* were the last person in need of liberation!' she declared.

In July Elaine Farrow came to stay with me again. She had a job working for an architect, an urbane, bearded man with the unlikely name of Gary Cooper. He had business in Auckland and Elaine accompanied him as his assistant. She slept at my flat and disappeared first thing every morning in the taxi that the attentive Mr Cooper sent for her.

Elaine and her family had now moved out of the motel unit into a small rented house near to Taupo. Now that she was working full time and financially independent, she was making plans for a surprise visit to the United Kingdom next Christmas. Meanwhile she threw herself energetically into her job, forever quoting her employer's sayings: 'Gary says this, Gary says that'. We made the most of what nightlife Auckland had to offer and I couldn't help wondering what the hell was going on.

On her last evening Gary took both of us out for dinner, followed by a visit to the cabaret at the Hotel Intercontinental.

Afterwards he insisted on taking Elaine and myself back to his motel on the North Shore, ostensibly for coffee. I didn't want to go because it was a long way from Mount Albert and I found Elaine's boss far too slick for my liking. I liked the idea of Elaine going with him alone even less, so I jumped into the taxi with as good a grace as I could muster.

We drank our coffee and talked for ages. Then he suggested that we both stay there for the night as it was very late and he couldn't be bothered to drive us home. I was furious but not surprised. When in a situation I don't like, I normally get up and walk away from it, but I couldn't walk away from this one because Elaine was already slipping out of her dress and getting into bed. In any case, I had barely enough cash on me for the taxi fare.

I performed an ill-natured striptease and also got into bed. To put it mildly, that night was one of the weirdest I have ever spent. The three of us shared the one room, in three single beds, which I reckoned was a very peculiar arrangement for a motel room, bearing in mind what one hears about motels. Gary, who was much given to deep analysis of himself and those around him, talked a great deal about the absent Mrs Cooper. Elaine talked about Michael. I'm not sure if my presence was required as a chaperone or not, but I fervently wished they would both shut up so that I might get some sleep.

In the morning, Gary drove us back to Mount Albert so that Elaine might collect her things before they returned to Taupo. They drove off together, laughing and waving. I have a very cynical mind and calculated that there were a great many more motels between Auckland and Taupo.

If Kathleen wondered where the three of us had been all night, she was left wondering; I had no intention of enlightening her.

Late one evening I made a phone call home to England. An old school friend was getting married that day and as it was doubtless too late to talk her out of it, I wanted to wish her well. Her younger sister answered the phone and at first hadn't got a blessed clue as to who was calling, but I persevered.

The penny dropped. 'Wendy? WENDY! Oh Christine, come quickly. It's Wendy. In New Zealand and she's got a funny accent.'

Her shrieks nearly deafened me. The bride came thumping down the stairs, breathlessly grabbed the receiver and promptly burst into tears. I howled too. It's nice to have a good bawl at a wedding even if one is on the other side of the globe. What followed was a disjointed conversation between both parties but I was able to gather she had been in the middle of having her face made up; now I had made her cry so much that the make-up lady would have to start all over again.

I made her promise to sent me a wedding photograph and hung up, hoping I hadn't made her late for the church.

In August, my flat-mate celebrated her twenty-first birthday and I gave her a bottle of wine with the highly optimistic intention of putting her into a good mood. The age of miracles is not dead – it worked. We had a couple of glasses each for our elevenses and a rare atmosphere of *bonhomie* prevailed for the rest of the day.

Kathleen's family were coming up from Kawerau to take her out for a special evening and Kathleen had been looking forward to it for weeks. She had made herself a new dress. The poor thing didn't have many clothes but what she had she made, and quite well too. For her birthday she had put together a black and white creation and I came home every afternoon to find her kneeling on the floor doing things with scissors and tailor's chalk, with half a dozen pins stuck between her teeth.

I never liked Kathleen. In fact I despised her because she was dull and so negative, but when it came to cutting out patterns and sewing, she left me standing. With practice I could just about thread a needle and sew on a button but that was my limit. My needlework teacher had despaired of me – to be honest most of my teachers had despaired of me, but the unfortunate woman who was faced with the disaster I made out of a simple cookery apron must have been tempted to resign on the spot.

Anne McCowan offered to do Kathleen's hair, which was dark, heavy and shoulder-length. Anne fiddled about for most of the afternoon with hairpins and grips, forcing the reluctant tresses into a *chignon*, which may have been stylish when Anne was living in Staines but made poor Kathleen look about forty. However, it was her birthday so I told her she looked very nice.

One morning after Kathleen's big day, I woke up with a hideously swollen face and a devastating toothache. I tried to examine my teeth in the bathroom mirror but couldn't open my mouth wide enough. Kathleen offered me the benefit of her vast medical experience with the advice, 'You should go to the dentist.'

'You don't say!' I replied nastily while trying to drink a cup of coffee out of the corner of my mouth. She no doubt meant well, but I was in a dangerous mood and liable to throw things.

The dentist in Avondale was next door to the bank – we frequently heard the sound of the drill coming through the wall – and I crawled up the stairs to his surgery first thing. Geraldine came too to make sure I got there. She shoved me into a seat in the waiting room and thrust some magazines on to my lap.

'Have you any idea how awful you look?' she offered by way of comfort. I nodded miserably.

'Well I'll pop back later to see how you're getting on. I expect we shall hear you yelling through the wall.'

'*Goodbye*, Geraldine.'

I was in and out of the dentist's chair for most of the morning. The trouble was due to an infected gum surrounding my wisdom tooth and my torturer in the clean white coat made an incision or two to drain off the poison. I only ever pray when I'm in trouble and I prayed for a merciful deliverance several times that morning. Eventually the gory business was over and I was sent away with a bill for twenty-five dollars and a mouthwash that tasted like turps.

My face was so stiff that I could hardly speak, a fact that my colleagues were quick to take advantage of, and I looked ghastly. All I need now is for Jan-Yves to turn up, I thought sourly, but during the afternoon, when I fainted in the banking hall (which looked bad for business) B.J. decided enough was enough and took me home in his car.

He escorted me to the door and told me not to come back until I was completely better. I thought to myself: 'if he dares to tell me that *she'll be right*, I'll hit him, I know I will.'

When he had gone, I took two aspirin and went to bed. Next day I looked almost human again but since I was still feeling delicate, I took B.J. at his word and stayed home. By the evening, though, I was sufficiently recovered to accompany Marie and Mariana Franklin to the opening lecture of 'Music Therapy for Handicapped Children', which Marie had been so busy organising. Richard was there too, on vacation and looking more handsome than ever, with a tan acquired from skiing in the Southern Alps.

The lecture proved to be informal and fascinating. The driving forces behind it, one a professor of music and the other a teacher of handicapped children at a school near Birmingham, England, had come together as a partnership some years earlier in order to help mentally retarded or handicapped children learn to communicate and co-ordinate their responses through the media of music and an understanding of basic rhythm. The motive behind the New Zealand tour was to train teachers and other interested parties in the methods that had proved so outstandingly successful. Out of over 1,500 children worked with, only three had failed to respond at all.

The tour became a notable success, due in the main to Marie Franklin's enthusiasm and organisational abilities.

In late September I attended another talk of quite a different sort, this one being about the psychic surgeons of the Philippines, a cult that was causing quite a furore in the popular press at the time. Melva Scott, who had contacts at all levels, managed to get hold of a naval captain and his wife who claimed to have first-hand experience of the phenomenon and were very willing to talk about it and show films, all in glorious Technicolor.

This bizarre activity originated in Manila, where the so-called surgeons performed complex operations using psychic powers that flowed into their hands without resorting to anaesthetics or surgical instruments. The patient remained conscious throughout and claimed to feel no pain whatsoever. No veins or arteries were severed so there was no shock and little or no bleeding. Assertions had been made of miraculous recoveries following the 'psychic' removal of cancerous growths or blood clots.

One film showed an operation, supposedly on an optic nerve, and involved the removal of the entire eyeball, which was placed tidily on the patient's cheek. At this point of high drama, the girl sitting next to me flopped out in a graceful swoon on the floor.

Melva materialised at my side in the darkened room. 'Can we get her to the "Ladies"?' she uttered in a stage whisper.

The poor girl was starting to come round so we half carried her between us and propped her up on a chair in the cloakroom, where she clutched feebly at my hand for support.

Melva said, 'I'd better get back. Can you manage?'

'Yes, Melva.'

And so I never saw the rest of the film show to learn the ultimate destiny of the eyeball on the cheek. Richard Franklin said that the whole thing was a load of nonsense and I was more than half inclined to agree.

But even so . . .

CHAPTER XV

Goodbye to New Zealand

'Do you realise, Kerry, that it's over a year now since we left England?' I announced with heavy significance. I was sprawled across her bed, watching her pack.

'Thirty-one, thirty-two, thirty-three . . . what did you say?' She paused in the removal of umpteen pairs of knickers from the drawer into a very expensive looking suitcase.

'I said, it's over a year since we first met.'

'Well, that's just wonderful. What are we supposed to do, go out and celebrate?' More counting. 'You know, I'm not going to get all this stuff in here, am I?' She absently patted the little piles again, like a loving mother cat doing a paw-count of her litter.

'You could always try being rational about it and dispose of the excess. After all, what's Ross going to say when you turn up with all this lot?' Kerry had finally acceded to her boyfriend's demands that she move in with him at St Helier. It was her last day living in the hotel and I had come to see her as I had some news of my own to impart.

'I've decided to go to Australia!'

'You're what?' She stared at me as if I had just announced I was off to sail across the Pacific on a raft.

I still felt slightly incredulous about it myself. Two days before, I had received Jan-Yves' letter issuing his ultimatum. It would soon be the start of the long summer vacation and he was planning on taking a trip up to Queensland. He didn't intend going alone (he wrote). With the letter was a cheque for the air fare.

'Get yourself over here or I shall come and get you.' I rather liked that bit.

It was six months since I had seen Jan-Yves and I was ready to react impulsively. I carefully put his cheque away, cashed some of my own money, and bought a ticket to Sydney.

I gave the bank a month's notice. 'So you see, I shall be leaving in November,' I said.

'But you didn't much like Sydney when we were there before,' Kerry protested.

I laughed, 'Well I shall like it well enough now!'

Kathleen's illogical reaction to my impending departure ran true to form. In view of the fact that we have never hit it off, I thought, at last I've done something that will please her – but not a bit of it. She initially sulked and then treated me to a vitriolic tirade on my numerous shortcomings, with dire predictions as to how I would come a cropper one of these days.

'Kathleen, I can see that *one of these days* you are going to make someone a lovely mother-in-law,' I replied with polite restraint.

Over the next days the situation did not improve. Marie Franklin kindly invited me to stay with them for my last weeks in Auckland and though at first I refused, after another twenty-four hours of Kathleen's surly silence – I didn't mind arguing but I objected to being ignored – I rang Marie back and gratefully accepted her offer. I said goodbye to Anne and Bob McCowan (Anne had finally forgiven me for the washing machine episode), threw my clothes into a couple of by now rather battered suitcases, and everything else into cardboard boxes. Les collected me and I moved into the house in Remuera.

It was lovely to be living in the atmosphere of a real home again. Marie put me in Richard's old room, now quite unnaturally tidy and devoid of its horrible bottled specimens and smelly trainers. There was a toy koala perched on a shelf and beneath it, the enlightening notice, *Yes folks, this IS a koala* in Richard's bold, scrawling hand.

Remuera is right across the city from Avondale and Les suggested that I take the small suburban train to work to avoid complicated bus changes. On my first Monday morning I duly went along to the station at nearby Newmarket and bought a ticket. When I reached the single platform, I saw the tail-end of a train disappearing up the line but I wasn't worried as I had plenty of time. I sat down to wait.

A quarter of an hour passed, and then a uniformed railway official came and stood a few yards away and regarded me quizzically.

'Would you be waiting for anything in particular, Miss?' he asked, rocking slowly on his heels.

He looked normal enough but you never can tell, so I thought I'd better humour him. 'Yes,' I said brightly. 'I'm waiting for a train actually.'

He folded his arms and stared at me very hard. 'Train's gone.'

'Yes I know, I'm waiting for the next one.'

'Well that, of course, is entirely up to you,' the man went on, 'except that there *isn't* another train. Not this morning.'

'But there has to be another train!'

'Why, because you say so?' My informant was beginning to enjoy himself and comprehension sluggishly began to dawn. This was definitely not the District Line.

The horrible man warmed to his subject. 'There are two trains in the morning, one at half past seven and one at eight. It is now,' he made a theatrical gesture of consulting his watch, 'eight-fifteen. The next train will depart at four o'clock . . .'

I didn't wait to hear any more but was halfway up the steps and heading in the direction of the nearest bus stop.

Ill-disguised mirth had been Les and Mariana's reaction that evening when I indignantly related my experience of the Auckland railway system and I can imagine only too well Philip's comment, had he been there: 'Silly Pom!'

The next two weeks flew by in a frenzy of packing and arrangements. I helped Melva Scott to organise a charity fashion show which raised two thousand dollars for a new ambulance station. There was a guest appearance by Miss New Zealand, who proved that some beautiful girls certainly are dumb as the poor thing had her jaw wired up following an accident while modelling on a motor bike.

At the last gathering I attended of the Women's Club I was presented with a gorgeous spray of orchids and a pendant made of New Zealand greenstone. Melva and her husband were going to Sydney too in a few weeks for a holiday so we made arrangements to meet.

I started some serious packing and was dismayed to find so much had accumulated in a year, including three toy poodles and a blonde wig. The poodles were hand-made in sheepskin by B.J.'s wife and dyed in bright colours. My three were orange, pink and white but the white one was my favourite and sat on my bed. I called him Monsieur Cognac. He and his two brothers went into the cabin trunk. The blonde wig I gave to Mariana. I was auburn and freckled and blonde hair did nothing for me; to be perfectly honest, it didn't do an awful lot for Mariana either but she cavorted around the house in it and insisted on wearing it out to flabbergast her boyfriend.

Her father commented that she looked like a witch.

Mariana had resumed teaching at last and was very busy. Most evenings, Marie's kitchen table was obliterated under bits of cardboard, old magazines, glue, scissors and the like as Mariana's inventive mind created various projects for school. I dragged her away from it one evening and we went to the cinema to see *The Sting*, which I considered to be over-long, though the music was nice.

As soon as I had made my decision to go to Australia, I had written and informed my parents and their reaction, in numerous, terse communiqués, had been disapproving to put it mildly. One afternoon I walked into the Franklin's kitchen to find both Marie and Mariana sitting at the table. Marie was shelling peas.

'I'm afraid I've got something to tell you and you're not going to like it,' she began. There was an uncomfortable pause. 'Wendy, I've had a letter from your mother.'

'Oh?'

'She's not at all happy about your going to Sydney.'

'She wasn't exactly overjoyed about my coming to New Zealand, but she got over it.'

As if acting on an unspoken cue, Mariana said, 'She's written to ask Mum to try and persuade you not to go but to get a flight straight back to the UK.'

I knew that I had heard her correctly but I still yelled, 'She WHAT?'

Marie looked unhappy. 'I must say it was a very strange letter. Your mother doesn't seem to think you'll be able to manage. She thinks it's high time you came home.'

Mariana giggled. 'We came to the conclusion that she doesn't know you very well.'

'Huh! I came to that conclusion when I was ten years old. Oh, how dare she! Marie, I'm sorry. It's not fair for you to be bothered with this.'

Writing behind my back to my dear friends, who had already done so much to make me welcome in a strange land! It was too much, and I erupted into a raging mood of self-pity and indignation. 'I will not be told what to do, not by her, and I shall certainly not be persuaded where I should go. I will go to Sydney, Timbuktu, anywhere I damn well please.'

'Yes, that's rather what we thought,' said Marie. She looked distressed by my outburst and I was instantly sorry. This was not my home and I had no right to screech like a demented fishwife in it. I had to get out so I asked Mariana if I might borrow her car.

'No way,' she said. 'You're in too much of a temper to drive. Go for one of your walks.'

I obeyed and it took the best part of an hour and the uphill slog to Auckland Domain before I had exorcised my temper tantrum and outrage. Then I saw the funny side of it: my mother's absurd notion that she could influence my decisions and the sadness of the fact that she had learned nothing in a year. I turned around to hurry back and continue with my packing.

With only a few more days to go, I began the round of goodbyes, the places first and then the people. Auckland's two most striking landmarks have to be Rangitoto Island and One Tree Hill, and I toiled up the summit of the latter to remember the view of the former. The Maori name of the hill is *Maungakiekie.* The solitary tree on the hill is a sturdy Scottish pine, put there to replace a native *totari* tree. Nowadays sheep graze peacefully on the lush terraces that were once part of a defensible Maori stronghold. The soaring stone summit was put there by the *pakeha* in honour of the dispossessed Maori people; it might have been better to have handed back their land.

Another day I went again to Auckland Domain and its beautiful area of parkland and trees, which affords the best view of the city and the Harbour. From there I could see the sleek, white lines of a

Farewell dinner at the Franklins'.

passenger liner in Prince's Wharf, the *Royal Viking Sun*. She was one of a new class of élite cruise ships, very fast and very expensive.

I thought sadly that I should probably never see the old *Ellinis* again.

Turning my back on the harbour, I could make out the turreted roof of Auckland Grammar School and beyond that, Mount Albert and the quiet western suburbs of Avondale, New Lynn, and Glen Eden, where Melva Scott lived.

I didn't go back to Mount Albert, nor did I go to Ponsonby. There wasn't enough time to make a trip to Waiheke but Waiheke was a place I wanted to remember, with the Franklin family there. I had no desire to make a last visit alone.

I embarked upon an orgy of souvenir buying: Maori dolls, greenstone jewellery and some calendar tea-towels for 1975. For Marie I bought a pair of hand-painted porcelain oil lamps. Kerry and I had one last meal together, shared two bottles of wine and made fervent promises to keep in touch. 'Though I'm not much of

Mariana and Les Franklin.

a letter writer,' she said (as if I needed reminding!). Cold intuition told me that had I been staying on in Auckland, my meetings with Kerry would have grown more and more infrequent. It was better this way. Even so, I was still unsure as to whether she had really been a friend or I a convenience, but I knew I would never forget her.

I went over to One Tree Hill to say goodbye to Frank and Eunice. Eunice was recovering from a bout of 'flu and lay wanly on the sofa, a box of tissues on her lap. I gave her some juicy home-grown oranges from the Franklin's garden that Marie had picked for her. Frank toasted my good health with a glass of sherry, made a touching little speech, and kissed me on the cheek.

Then it was my last day.

I certainly didn't earn my keep on that final day at the bank, but wasted a great deal of time on the phone and chatting to my favourite customers over the counter. At about five o'clock we all went into the staff room to have a party, because Avondale, like Mount Albert, was a 'dry' district without a single pub. Someone had brought in a cassette recorder and the beer flowed freely. I took silly photos of everybody and flirted outrageously with B.J., who, now that I was leaving, suddenly seemed rather sweet and appealing.

Mr Evans the Manager came out of his office and said all the usual things: sorry to be losing you, wish you all the best, and then presented me with a superb book of New Zealand photography.

Someone – I expect it was B.J. – put me into a taxi when I left to go home because I had so much to carry. Quite probably I couldn't walk in a straight line either. Marie had excelled herself that evening for our last meal together. I gave her the little oil lamps and we sat talking around the table over our coffee for a long time afterwards. I was forbidden to help with the washing up, so I went outside to stand on the roof patio. It was very nearly dark but I could just make out the familiar hump of Rangitoto in the distance. Somewhere beyond it lay Waiheke.

I went back inside to sit in the lounge, where there was an open log fire burning, for although the days were warming up, it was still chilly at night. Les came in, lit up his pipe and disappeared behind the evening newspaper. I leaned back in my chair and thought, 'This time tomorrow I shall be with Jan-Yves.' I was sad to be leaving and yet eager to be gone, for this was just one segment of my life that I had outgrown, seemingly overnight.

I went to bed very late and hardly slept at all. I had booked a taxi to take me to the airport but I had reckoned without the Franklin family, up and dressed at the crack of dawn.

'We saw you into the country and we'll see you out of it,' said Les as he loaded my cases into the boot of the car.

My flight was scheduled for eight o'clock but of course I had to be there at least an hour earlier. There had been heavy rain during the night and the sky still looked depressingly overcast and grey. We sat round in the airport lounge waiting for my flight number to be called while I grew more tense with every passing minute. I had turned my back on England coldly enough, but I discovered that leaving New Zealand was not so easy. I delved into my bag for Jan-Yves' last letter, that I always carried around with me, and read it for the umpteenth time. *I wonder if he's still got his beard?*

Then Mariana was poking me. 'That's your flight. Come on!'

I stood up, collected my things together, and kissed my friends goodbye. When I reached the final departure gate, I turned round for the last time and the three of them were still standing there, Marie, Les and Mariana. Mariana smiled encouragingly. 'Good luck!' she called. I waved back awkwardly, encumbered with bags on each arm, and stepped out on to the oily black, wet tarmac, taking care to avoid the worst of the puddles.

I must come back here one day to this very special place, I told myself while the plane accelerated for its take-off. Once airborne, it circled just once and I caught a fleeting glimpse of the sea between the clouds.

Moments later, above the cloud level, the sun was shining brilliantly on what promised to be a perfect spring day.

Epilogue

Essex, England

It is Christmas Day 1984 and my children are dancing around the house, noisily chanting '*Feed the W-o-r-l-d*'. I have just spoken to Marie Franklin in New Zealand on the phone, as I have done every Christmas since I have been home. Les passed away two years ago but Marie has her family with her for the holiday. Philip and Mariana are both married; Philip has three children and Mariana has a daughter. Richard has qualified as a doctor and is practising in Hong Kong.

Before me on the desk are three photographs, two of them taken in New Zealand. One is of Les, Marie and myself, taken on my very first weekend in Auckland during the visit we made to Takapuna beach; the other was taken eleven years ago today exactly, my Christmas spent with the Franklin family. I carefully replace these two pictures with the others in the album.

The third photograph is of a blond, long-haired young man taken in the dazzling Australian sunshine. I look at this picture for a long time before carefully propping it up where I can easily see it.

Jan-Yves.